POP CHORD SONG BOOK THREE

This publication is not authorised for sale in the United States of America and/or Canada.

Wise Publications
London/New York/Paris/Sydney/Copenhagen/Madrid

Exclusive Distributors:
Music Sales Limited
8/9 Frith Street,
London W1V 5TZ, England.
Music Sales Pty Limited
120 Rothschild Avenue,
Rosebery, NSW 2018,
Australia.

Order No. AM957913
ISBN 0-7119-7402-0
This book © Copyright 1999 by Wise Publications
www.internetmusicshop.com

Unauthorised reproduction of any part of this publication by any means including photocopying is an infringement of copyright.

Compiled by Peter Evans
New music arrangements by James Dean
Music processed by The Pitts

Cover design by Chloë Alexander
Photographs courtesy of London Features International

Printed in the United Kingdom by Caligraving Limited,
Thetford, Norfolk.

Your Guarantee of Quality:
As publishers, we strive to produce every book to the highest commercial standards. This book has been carefully designed to minimise awkward page turns and to make playing from it a real pleasure.
Particular care has been given to specifying acid-free, neutral-sized paper made from pulps which have not been elemental chlorine bleached. This pulp is from farmed sustainable forests and was produced with special regard for the environment. Throughout,
the printing and binding have been planned to ensure a sturdy, attractive publication which should give years of enjoyment.
If your copy fails to meet our high standards, please inform us and we will gladly replace it.

Music Sales' complete catalogue describes thousands of titles and is available in full colour sections by subject, direct from Music Sales Limited. Please state your areas of interest and send a cheque/postal order for £1.50 for postage to: Music Sales Limited, Newmarket Road, Bury St. Edmunds, Suffolk IP33 3YB.

All That I Need *Boyzone* 5

Because We Want To *Billie* 8

Cruel Summer *Ace Of Base* 11

Dreams *The Corrs* 14

Each Time *E-17* 16

Got The Feelin' *Five* 19

Immortality *Celine Dion & The Bee Gees* 22

Killing Me Softly *The Fugees* 24

Let Me Entertain You *Robbie Williams* 26

Miami *Will Smith* 29

One For Sorrow *Steps* 32

Stop *Spice Girls* 46

Thank U *Alanis Morissette* 34

This Is Hardcore *Pulp* 36

Torn *Natalie Imbruglia* 38

Until The Time Is Through *Five* 41

You Don't Care About Us *Placebo* 44

Playing Guide: Relative Tuning/Reading Chord Boxes 4

Relative Tuning

The guitar can be tuned with the aid of pitch pipes or dedicated electronic guitar tuners which are available through your local music dealer. If you do not have a tuning device, you can use relative tuning. Estimate the pitch of the 6th string as near as possible to E or at least a comfortable pitch (not too high, as you might break other strings in tuning up). Then, while checking the various positions on the diagram, place a finger from your left hand on the:

5th fret of the E or 6th string and **tune the open A** (or 5th string) to the note (A)

5th fret of the A or 5th string and **tune the open D** (or 4th string) to the note (D)

5th fret of the D or 4th string and **tune the open G** (or 3rd string) to the note (G)

4th fret of the G or 3rd string and **tune the open B** (or 2nd string) to the note (B)

5th fret of the B or 2nd string and **tune the open E** (or 1st string) to the note (E)

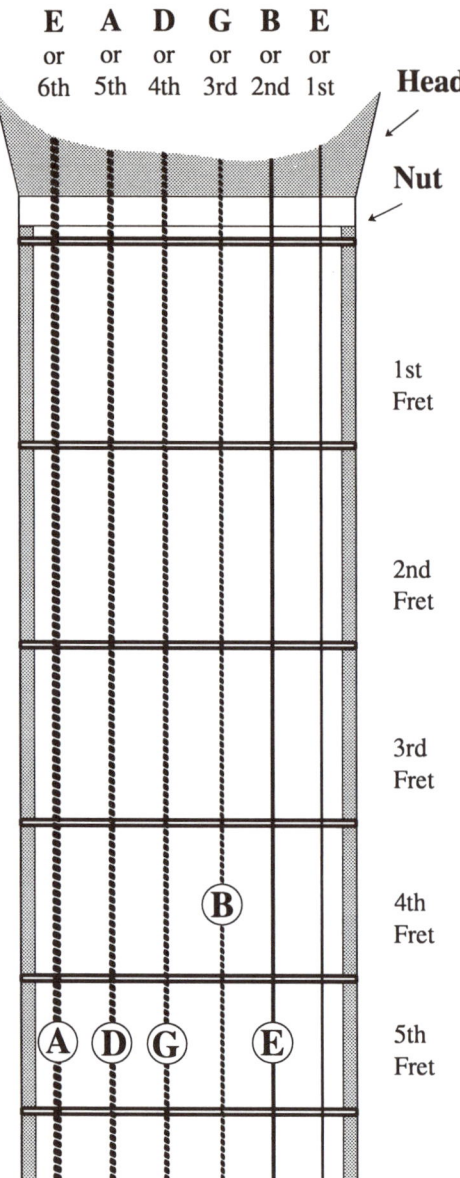

Reading Chord Boxes

Chord boxes are diagrams of the guitar neck viewed head upwards, face on as illustrated. The top horizontal line is the nut, unless a higher fret number is indicated, the others are the frets.

The vertical lines are the strings, starting from E (or 6th) on the left to E (or 1st) on the right.

The black dots indicate where to place your fingers.

Strings marked with an O are played open, not fretted.

Strings marked with an X should not be played.

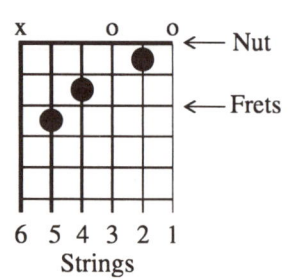

All That I Need

Words & Music by
Evan Rogers & Carl Sturken

[Chord diagrams: C, G, Am7, Dm7, G11, Am, F, B♭maj7]

Intro | C | G | Am7 | Dm7 G11 ||

Verse 1
      C   G
I was lost and alone
        Am7
Trying to grow,
          Dm7   G11   C
Making my way down that long winding road.
         G
Had no reason or rhyme
       Am7
Like a song out of time
       Dm7   G11   C
And there you are standing in front of my eyes.
       G
How could I be such a fool
   Am7   Dm7 G
To let go of love and break all the rules?
C   G
Girl, when you walked out that door
   Am7   Dm7   G11
Left a hole in my heart and now I know for sure.

Chorus 1
     C   G
You're the air that I breathe,
      Am7
Girl, you're all that I need,
      Dm7   G11
And I wanna thank you lady.
   C   G
You're the words that I read,
      Am7
You're the light that I see,
     Dm7   G11
And your love is all that I need.

© Copyright 1995 Bayjun Beat Music/Music Corporation of America, USA.
MCA Music Limited, 77 Fulham Palace Road, London W6.
All Rights Reserved. International Copyright Secured.

Link | C | G | Am7 | Dm7 G11 ‖

Verse 2
        C   G
I was searching in vain,
             Am7
Playing your game
           Dm7   G11   C
Had no-one else but myself left to blame.
             G
You came into my world,
          Am7
No diamonds or pearls
        Dm7   G11   C
Could ever replace what you gave to me, girl.

Prechorus 2
      C   G
Just like a castle of sand,
         Am7
Girl, I almost let love
    Dm7   G
Slip right out of my hand.
  C   G
And just like a flower needs rain
      Am7
I will stand by your side
       Dm7   G11
Through the joy and the pain.

Chorus 2

    C   G
You're the air that I breathe,
        Am7
Girl, you're all that I need,
     Dm7 G11
And I wanna thank you lady
C   G
you're the words that I read,
       Am7
You're the light that I see
     Dm7 G11
And your love is all that I need.

Instr. Solo | Am | F | B♭maj7 | Dm7 G11 ||

Chorus 3 As Chorus 1

Coda

    C   G
You're the song that I sing,
       Am7
Girl, you're my everything
     Dm7 G11
And I wanna thank you lady.
C
You're all that I needed, girl,
G
You're the air that I breathe, yeah
Am7   Dm7 G11
And I wanna thank you, lady. *Repeat to fade*

Because We Want To

Words & Music by
Dion Rambo, Jacques Richmond, Wendy Page & James Marr

Intro

N.C.
We can do anything that we want,

We can do anything that we want,

We can do anything that we want,

We can do anything that we want.

Chorus 1

A
Why you gotta play that song so loud?

C#m
(Because we want to! Because we want to!)

A
Why you always run around in crowds?

C#m
(Because we want to! Because we want to!)

A
Why do you always have to dance all night?

C#m
(Because we want to! Because we want to!)

A
Why d'ya always say what's on your mind?

C#m
(Because we want to! Because we want to!)

Verse 1

      Amaj7 B   **C#m**
Don't try to tell me what I already know,

      Amaj7 B   **C#m**
Don't criticise me 'cause I'm runnin' the show.

      Amaj7 B   **G#m7/B C#m**
Some revolu - tion is gonna happen today,

  Amaj7   **B**
I'm gonna chase the dark clouds away,

C#m
Come on and help me sing it.

© Copyright 1998 Homeless Youth Music, Scu Music & Chrysalis Music Limited.
Administered by Chrysalis Music Limited, Bramley Road, London W10.
All Rights Reserved. International Copyright Secured.

Pre-chorus 1

   F♯m9 G♯m7   C♯m
We can do what we want to do,

We can do anything.
Amaj7 **G♯m7** **F♯m7**
Free to be who we want to be,
  G♯m7
Just tell yourself you can do it.

Chorus 2 As Chorus 1

Verse 2

     Amaj7 **B** **C♯m**
I'll throw a par - ty __ for the world and my friends,
     Amaj7 **B** **C♯m**
We'll take life eas - y __ the music never ends.
     Amaj7 **B** **G♯m7/B** **C♯m**
Perfect solu - tion to the stress and the strain,
 Amaj7   **B**
I know the sun will follow the rain,
C♯m
 Come on and help me sing it.

Pre-chorus 2 As Pre-chorus 1

Chorus 3 As Chorus 1

Middle | **A** | **C♯m** | **A** | **C♯m** |

  A
So shake it, move it, use the groove,
  C♯m
Go __ with the flow and take over the show
       A
And let me say it's sweet and it's an upbeat.
C♯m
Me and the crew, there's nothing we can do.

A   **C♯m**
Hey hey hey, hey hey hey.
     A
If you wanna catch this vibe then get with us,
C♯m
 Come on and help me sing it.

Pre-chorus 3
    F♯m9   **G♯m7**   **C♯m**
We can do what we want to do,

We can do anything.
Amaj7 **G♯m7**   **F♯m7**
Free to be who we want to be,
     G♯m7
Just tell yourself you can do it.

Chorus 4
      A
𝄆 Why you gotta play that song so loud?
       C♯m
(Because we want to! Because we want to!)
A
Why you always run around in crowds?
       C♯m
(Because we want to! Because we want to!)
      A
Why do you always have to dance all night?
       C♯m
(Because we want to! Because we want to!)
      A
Why d'ya always say what's on your mind?
       C♯m
(Because we want to! Because we want to!) 𝄇   *Repeat to fade*

Cruel Summer

**Words & Music by
Steve Jolley, Tony Swain, Siobhan Fahey, Keren Woodward & Sarah Dallin**

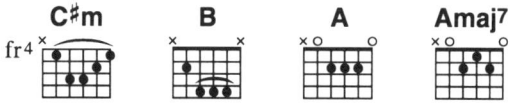

	C#m	B	A	C#m
Intro				

```
        C#m  B    A  B  C#m
             Mm,_____

        B     A  B  C#m
         Ah,_____

        B     A  B  C#m
         Mm,_____

        B     A  B
         Ah,_____
```

Verse 1
```
       C#m
       Hot summer streets
        B              A          B
       And the pavements are burning,
        C#m   B  A  B
       I sit around
       C#m          B        A
       Trying to smile, but the air
                B      C#m B A B
       Is so heavy and dry.
```

Verse 2
```
       C#m        B           A
          Strange voices are singing,
           B        C#m
       Ah, what did they say?
            B  A      B A B
       Things I can't understand.
           C#m           B
       It's too close for comfort,
               A           B       Amaj7 B A B
       This heat has got right out of hand.
```

© Copyright 1983 Broadley Music International & Associated Music International.
In A Bunch Music Limited (50%), PolyGram Music Publishing Limited,
47 British Grove, London W4 (25%) & Sony/ATV Music Limited,
10 Great Marlborough Street, London W1 (25%).
All Rights Reserved. International Copyright Secured.

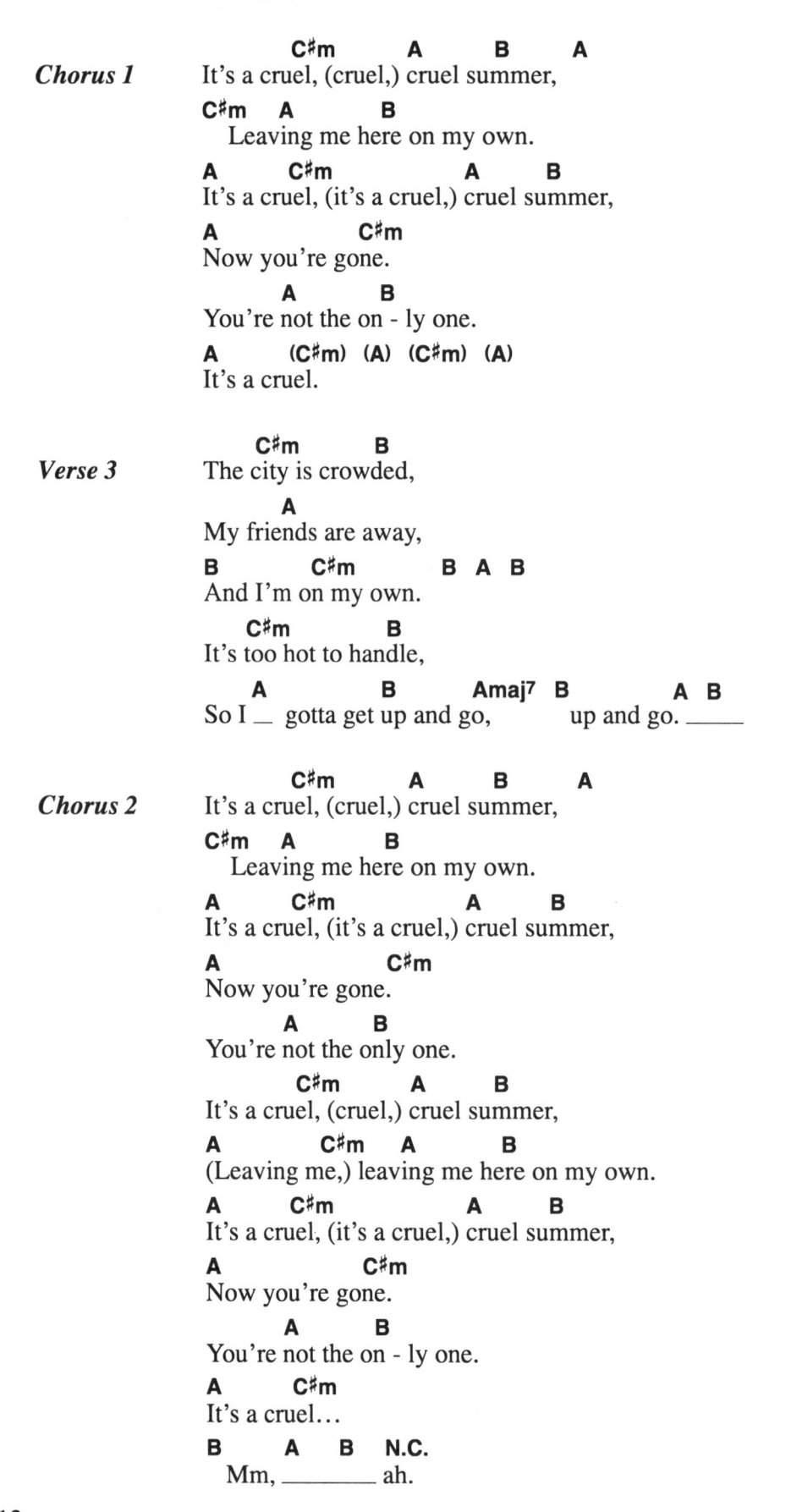

Chorus 1

        C#m   A   B   A
It's a cruel, (cruel,) cruel summer,

C#m   A   B
  Leaving me here on my own.

A   C#m   A   B
It's a cruel, (it's a cruel,) cruel summer,

A   C#m
Now you're gone.

     A   B
You're not the on - ly one.

   A   (C#m) (A) (C#m) (A)
It's a cruel.

Verse 3

    C#m   B
The city is crowded,

   A
My friends are away,

B   C#m   B A B
And I'm on my own.

  C#m   B
It's too hot to handle,

  A   B   Amaj7 B   A B
So I _ gotta get up and go,   up and go. _____

Chorus 2

     C#m   A   B   A
It's a cruel, (cruel,) cruel summer,

C#m A   B
  Leaving me here on my own.

A   C#m   A   B
It's a cruel, (it's a cruel,) cruel summer,

A   C#m
Now you're gone.

   A   B
You're not the only one.

   C#m   A   B
It's a cruel, (cruel,) cruel summer,

A   C#m A   B
(Leaving me,) leaving me here on my own.

A   C#m   A   B
It's a cruel, (it's a cruel,) cruel summer,

A   C#m
Now you're gone.

   A   B
You're not the on - ly one.

A   C#m
It's a cruel…

B   A   B N.C.
Mm, _____ ah.

Middle

      C♯m   A   B
Now don't you leave me, mm,
            A
Now don't you leave me,
   C♯m   A
Now don't you leave me.
    B   A
Come on, come on.
   C♯m   A   B
Now don't you leave me, mm,
        A
Now don't you leave me,
  Amaj⁷   B
Now don't you leave me,
     Amaj⁷ B
Come on,   come on.

Chorus 3

          C♯m   A   B
It's a cruel, (cruel,) cruel summer,
A   C♯m A   B
(Leaving me,) leaving me here on my own.
A   C♯m   A   B
It's a cruel, (it's a cruel,) cruel summer,
A   C♯m
Now you're gone.
     A   B
You're not the on - ly one.
A   C♯m   A   B   A C♯m A
It's a cruel, (cruel,) cruel summer,
     B   A C♯m
It's a cruel summer.
           A   B   A C♯m A
(It's a cruel,) cruel summer,
     B   A C♯m
It's a cruel summer.

Dreams

Words & Music by
Stevie Nicks

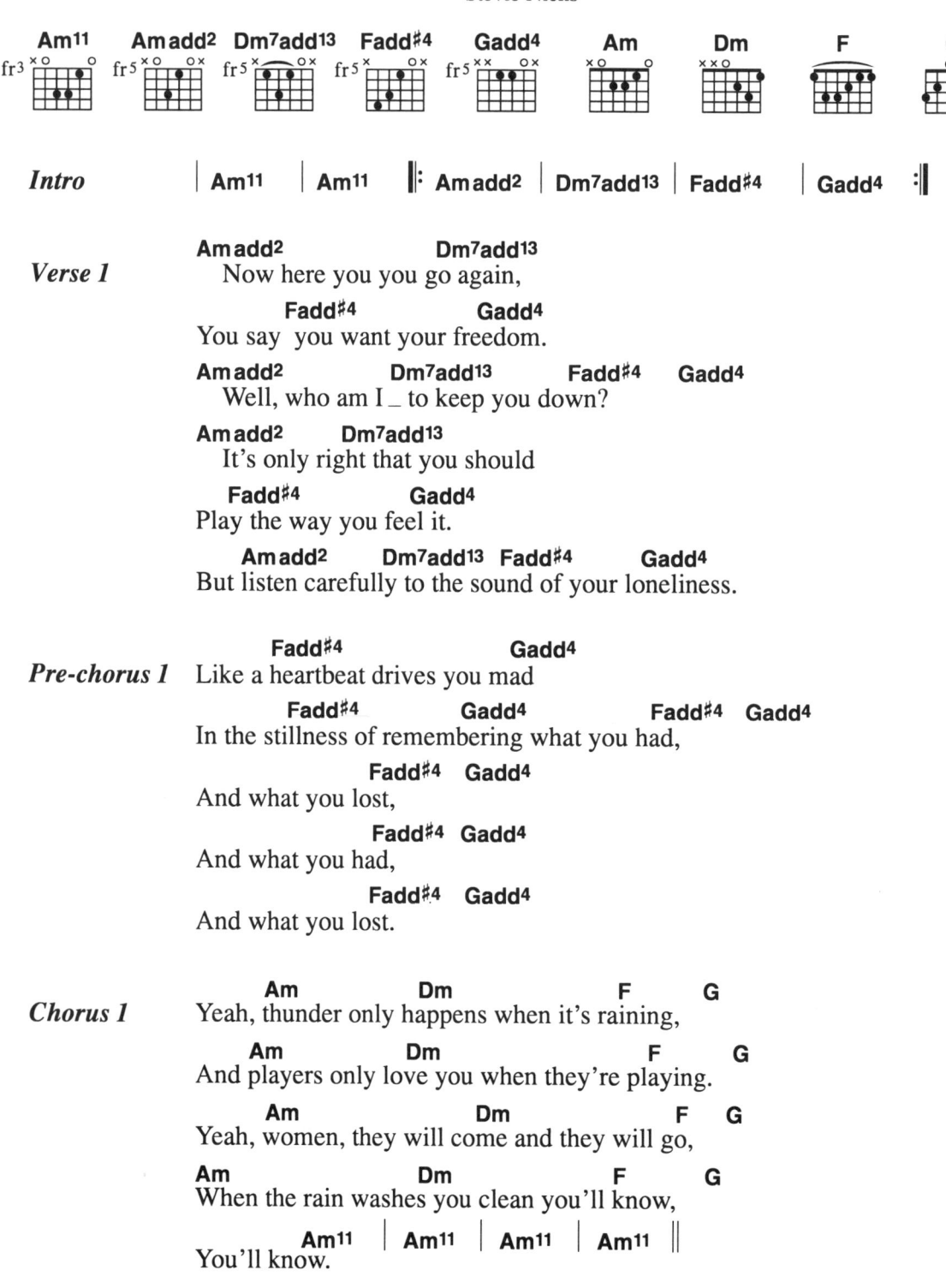

Am11 Amadd2 Dm7add13 Fadd#4 Gadd4 Am Dm F G

Intro | Am11 | Am11 |: Amadd2 | Dm7add13 | Fadd#4 | Gadd4 :|

Verse 1
     Amadd2   Dm7add13
Now here you you go again,
   Fadd#4   Gadd4
You say you want your freedom.
   Amadd2   Dm7add13   Fadd#4   Gadd4
Well, who am I _ to keep you down?
   Amadd2   Dm7add13
It's only right that you should
  Fadd#4   Gadd4
Play the way you feel it.
    Amadd2   Dm7add13 Fadd#4   Gadd4
But listen carefully to the sound of your loneliness.

Pre-chorus 1
   Fadd#4   Gadd4
Like a heartbeat drives you mad
   Fadd#4   Gadd4   Fadd#4 Gadd4
In the stillness of remembering what you had,
   Fadd#4 Gadd4
And what you lost,
     Fadd#4 Gadd4
And what you had,
    Fadd#4 Gadd4
And what you lost.

Chorus 1
     Am   Dm   F   G
Yeah, thunder only happens when it's raining,
   Am   Dm   F   G
And players only love you when they're playing.
     Am   Dm   F   G
Yeah, women, they will come and they will go,
  Am   Dm   F   G
When the rain washes you clean you'll know,
    Am11 | Am11 | Am11 | Am11 ||
You'll know.

© Copyright 1977 Welsh Witch Music, USA.
Sony/ATV Music Publishing, 10 Great Marlborough Street, London W1.
All Rights Reserved. International Copyright Secured.

| Amadd2 | Dm7add13 | Fadd#4 | Gadd4 ||

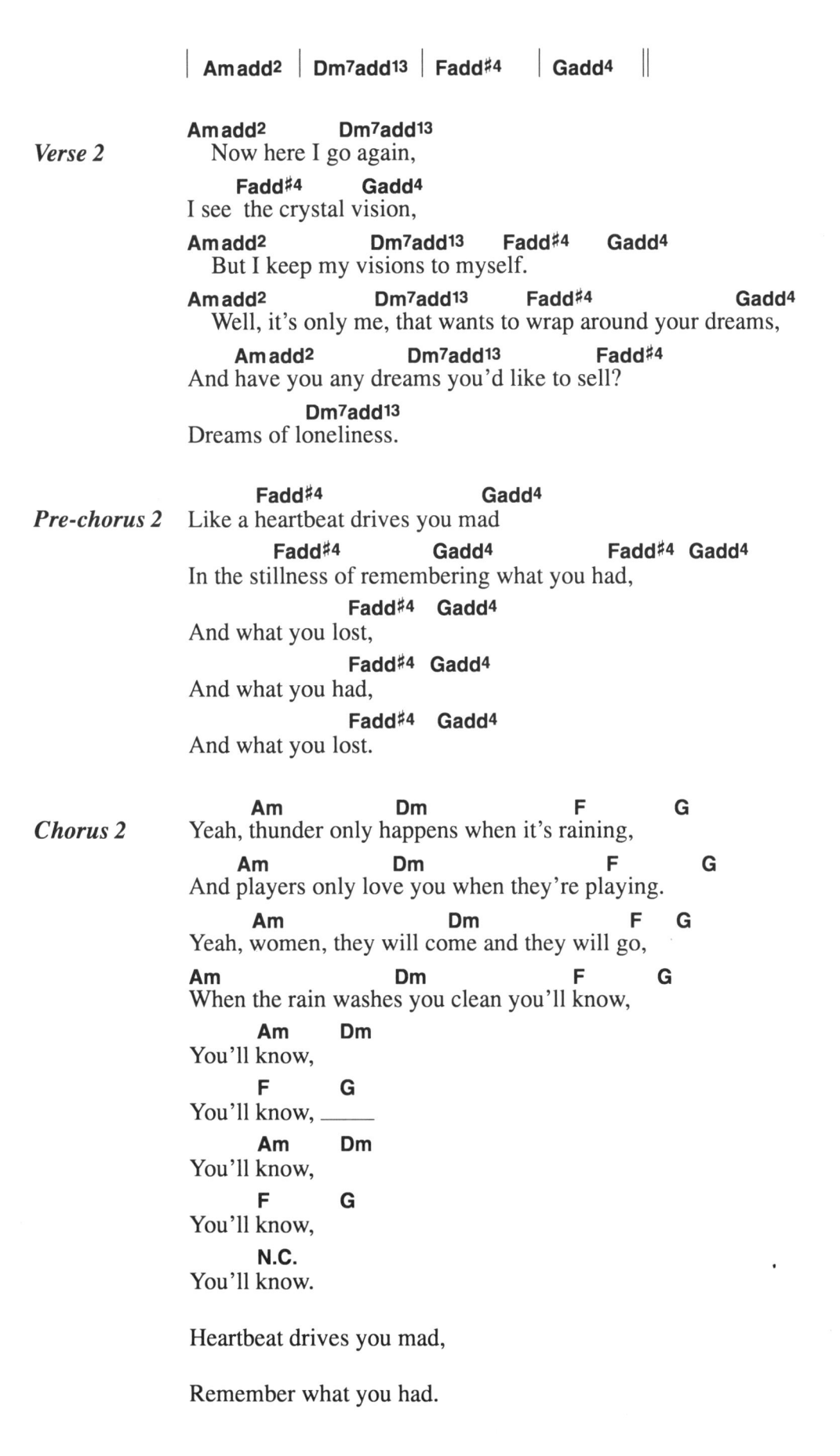

Verse 2

    Amadd2   Dm7add13
Now here I go again,
    Fadd#4   Gadd4
I see the crystal vision,
    Amadd2   Dm7add13   Fadd#4   Gadd4
But I keep my visions to myself.
    Amadd2   Dm7add13   Fadd#4   Gadd4
Well, it's only me, that wants to wrap around your dreams,
      Amadd2   Dm7add13   Fadd#4
And have you any dreams you'd like to sell?
          Dm7add13
Dreams of loneliness.

Pre-chorus 2

    Fadd#4   Gadd4
Like a heartbeat drives you mad
     Fadd#4   Gadd4   Fadd#4 Gadd4
In the stillness of remembering what you had,
     Fadd#4 Gadd4
And what you lost,
     Fadd#4 Gadd4
And what you had,
     Fadd#4 Gadd4
And what you lost.

Chorus 2

     Am   Dm   F   G
Yeah, thunder only happens when it's raining,
    Am   Dm   F   G
And players only love you when they're playing.
    Am   Dm   F G
Yeah, women, they will come and they will go,
Am   Dm   F   G
When the rain washes you clean you'll know,
    Am   Dm
You'll know,
    F   G
You'll know, _____
    Am   Dm
You'll know,
    F   G
You'll know,
    N.C.
You'll know.

Heartbeat drives you mad,

Remember what you had.

Each Time

Words & Music by
Brian Harvey, John Hendy, Terry Coldwell, Mark Reid, Ivor Reid & Jon Beckford

[Chord diagrams: B, G♯m7, D♯m7, Eadd2, D♯m, Gmaj7, Aadd2, F♯11, F♯m7, Em9, G11, C, Am7, Em7, Fadd2]

Intro | B | G♯m7 ||

D♯m7
   Please come back,
Eadd2   B   G♯m7
   I miss you baby, come on each time,
D♯m   Eadd2
   Oh yeah,
B
   Come on each time,
G♯m7
   I said you blow my mind,
D♯m7   Eadd2
   Oh yeah, ooh.

Verse 1
          B   G♯m7
Have you heard of a saying that those who are paying?
      D♯m7   Eadd2
You don't know what you got till it's gone.
      B   G♯m7
Well, there was my calling, I knew I was falling
   D♯m7   Eadd2
Into something that would be so wrong.
   Gmaj7
But I got hold of myself

And changed for the better,
   Aadd2
I can't get you out of my mind.
   Gmaj7
'Cause something inside
                         F♯11
Made me realise you were fine.

© Copyright 1998 Strongsongs Limited (50%) & Porky Publishing/
PolyGram Music Publishing Limited, 47 British Grove, London W4 (50%).
All Rights Reserved. International Copyright Secured.

Chorus 1   **B**
Each time when we're alone,
      G♯m7   **D♯m7**
I guess I didn't know how far we were apart.
                  Eadd2
Should have spoken to my heart.
  B
I guess I didn't know
         G♯m7   **D♯m7**
That each time you go away I'd cry.
  Eadd2   **B**
Oh, I can't take all these good-byes.

Verse 2   **G♯m7**
I know from this feeling inside there's a feeling,
D♯m7   **Eadd2**
I know that I'm in control.
 B   **G♯m7**
Everyday I am yearning, this love I feel burning,
D♯m7   **Eadd2**
Burning right through my soul.
  Gmaj7
So let's make the start
                  Aadd2
Of something that cannot be broken

The mould is so strong.
  Gmaj7
Treat this love as a child
                    F♯11
Then grows into something worthwhile.

Chorus 2   **B**
Each time when we're alone,
      G♯m7   **D♯m7**
I guess I didn't know how far we were apart.
                  Eadd2
Should have spoken to my heart.
  B
I guess I didn't know
         G♯m7   **D♯m7**
That each time you go away I'd cry.
  Eadd2
Oh, I can't take all these goodbyes.

Middle

Gmaj7
Deep love, so deep,
F♯m7
Deep love, so deep, yeah,
Gmaj7   **F♯m7**
  I can't take all these good-byes.
    Gmaj7
Gratefully I will be,
    F♯m7
You will see, please believe me.
  Em2   **F♯11**   **G11**
Oh, I can't take all these good-byes. _____

Chorus 3

                C
Each time when we're alone,
    Am7   **Em7**
I guess I didn't know how far we were apart.
              Fadd2
Should have spoken to my heart.
    C
I guess I didn't know,
    Am7   **Em7**
Each time you go away I'll cry.
  Fadd2
Oh, I can't take all these…

Repeat Chorus ad lib. to fade

Got The Feelin'

Words & Music by Richard Stannard, Julian Gallagher,
Sean Conlon, Jason Brown & Richard Breen

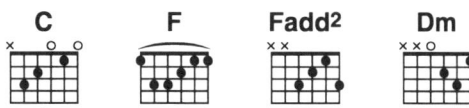

Intro
```
     C           F
|: Na na na, na _ na na,
   C           F
Na na na, na _ na na na. :|  Play 4 times
```

Verse 1
```
      C              F
Here we go again with the beats,
                    C                        F
We got your heads boppin' now you're talking from your seats.
                         C
If this is what you're wantin' over there,
F
Throw your hands up in the air,
         C                          F
Because you know we bring the sound so unique.
              C                     F
Now ev'rybody's movin' 'n' ev'rybody's groovin',
              C                F
Gettin' down with Five when we come your way.
               C                    F
Move it to the left, now you shake it to the right,
                      C                           F
Because you know we gotta keep this party boppin' through the night.

Check me out. Yo!
```

Pre-chorus 1
```
        C              F
Seven six five four three two one,
          C                     F
I'm on the microphone, got ya hot like the sun.
         C                          F
So a-one two three, now I'm waiting on the four,
        C                            F
Kick down the door and turn it up a little more.
```

Chorus 1	C F

Chorus 1

        C   F
If you've got the feelin', jump up to the ceilin',
     C   F
Oh, we're gettin' down tonight.
         C   F
And one if you're gonna, two if you wanna,
    C   F
Three 'cos ev'rything's alright.
        C   F
If you've got the feelin', less of the dreamin',
     C   F
Oh, we're gettin' down tonight.
        C   F
It's just 'round the corner, tell me if you wanna,
      C   F
Five will make you feel alright.

Link

| C Fadd2 | C Fadd2 ‖

Verse 2

  C   F
Move it at the back to the track,
         C   F
We got it going on, we're the leaders of the pack.
        C
And if you feel alright, hold it tight,
F
See we wanna carry on,
      C   F
'Cos we're gonna take you through into the dawn.
        C   F
Now everybody's movin', everybody's groovin',
       C   F
Gettin' down with Five when we come your way.
        C   F
So raise up your arms, as we drop it on the one,
            C   F
You see we're gonna carry on because the fun has just begun.

Check us out. Yo!

Pre-chorus 2   As Pre-chorus 1

Chorus 2   As Chorus 1

C Dm C Dm   C Dm C Dm
Oh, _____   oh, _____

Middle

     C   F
Na na na, na — na na,

     C   F
Na na na, na — na na na.

     C   F
Na na na, na — na na,

     C   F
Na na na, na — na na na.

     C   Fadd2
Na na na, na — na na,

     C   Fadd2
Na na na, na — na na na.

     C   Fadd2
Na na na, na — na na,

     C   Fadd2
Na na na, na — na na na.

Chorus 3

          C   Fadd2
If you've got the feelin', jump up to the ceilin',

     C   Fadd2
Oh, we're gettin' down tonight.

        C   Fadd2
And one if you're gonna, two if you wanna,

      C   Fadd2
Three 'cos ev'rything's alright.

          C   Fadd2
If you've got the feelin', less of the dreamin',

     C   Fadd2
Oh, we're gettin' down tonight.

         C   Fadd2
It's just 'round the corner, tell me if you wanna,

      N.C.
Five will make you feel alright.

Chorus 4   As Chorus 1

Chorus 5   As Chorus 3

Immortality

Words & Music by
Barry Gibb, Robin Gibb & Maurice Gibb

[Chord diagrams: D, A/C#, G/B, A, Bm, Em, G, F#m, E]

Intro | D | D | D |

    A/C# G/B D   A   Bm
So this is who I am, and this is all I know,
                         Em
And I must choose to live for all that I can give,

The spark that makes the power grow.

Verse 1

            D   A   G   F#m
And I will stand for my dream if I can,
G   D   Em   Bm
Symbol of my faith in who I am,
          Em
But you are my on - ly.
                D   A   G   F#m
And I must follow on the road that lies ahead,
G   D   Em   Bm
And I won't let my heart control my head,
          Em
But you are my on - ly.

Link 1

               D
And we don't say good-bye,
A   Bm
 We don't say good-bye,
E   Em
 And I know what I've got to be.

Chorus 1

D   Em F#m Em
Immor - tali - ty, —
D   Em   F#m Em
I make my journey through etern-i-ty,
D   Em   F#m   Em
I keep the memory of you and me inside.

© Copyright 1997 Gibb Brothers Music.
All Rights Reserved. International Copyright Secured.

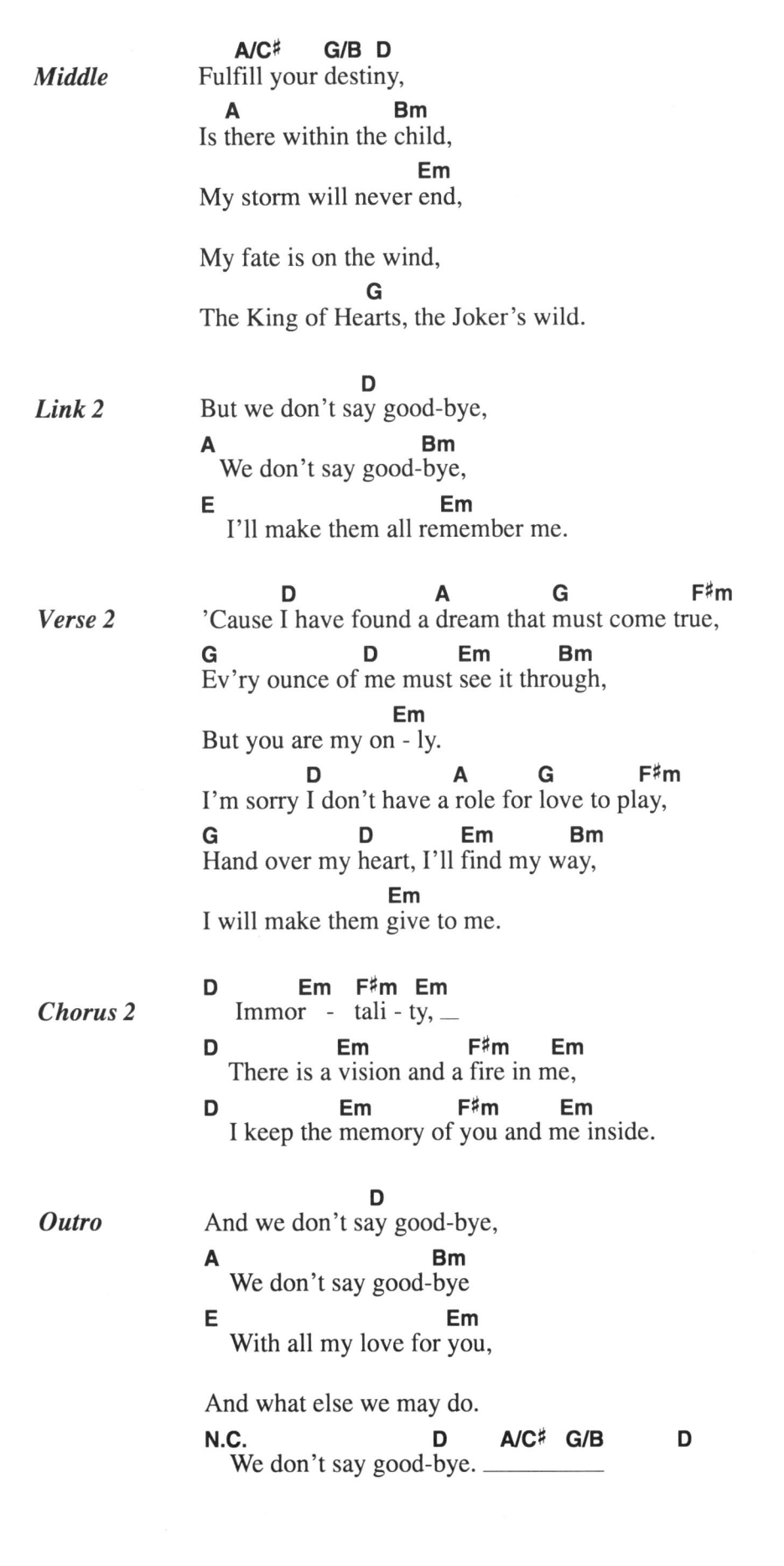

Middle

       A/C♯   G/B D
Fulfill your destiny,

   A   Bm
Is there within the child,

                      Em
My storm will never end,

My fate is on the wind,

            G
The King of Hearts, the Joker's wild.

Link 2

             D
But we don't say good-bye,

A   Bm
  We don't say good-bye,

E   Em
  I'll make them all remember me.

Verse 2

        D   A   G   F♯m
'Cause I have found a dream that must come true,

G   D   Em   Bm
Ev'ry ounce of me must see it through,

            Em
But you are my on - ly.

        D   A   G   F♯m
I'm sorry I don't have a role for love to play,

G   D   Em   Bm
Hand over my heart, I'll find my way,

            Em
I will make them give to me.

Chorus 2

D   Em F♯m Em
  Immor - tali - ty, __

D   Em   F♯m   Em
  There is a vision and a fire in me,

D   Em   F♯m   Em
  I keep the memory of you and me inside.

Outro

             D
And we don't say good-bye,

A   Bm
  We don't say good-bye

E   Em
  With all my love for you,

And what else we may do.

N.C.   D   A/C♯ G/B   D
  We don't say good-bye. _____

Killing Me Softly With His Song

Words by Norman Gimbel.
Music by Charles Fox

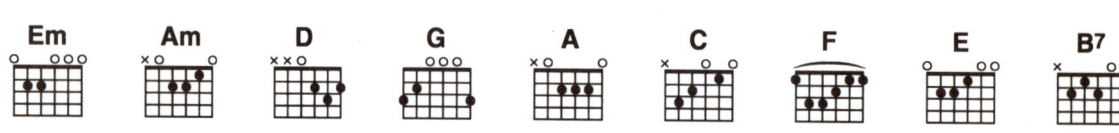

Chorus 1
    (Em)   (Am)
Strumming my pain with his fin - gers,
 (D)   (G)
Singing my life with his words,
 (Em)   (A)
Killing me softly with his song,
               (D)   (C)
Killing me soft - ly with his song,
             (G)   (C)
Telling my whole life with his words,
      (F)   (E)
Killing me softly with his song.

Link
Drum rhythm for 8 bars

Verse 1
(Am)   (D)
  I heard he sang a good song,
(G)   (C)
  I heard he had a smile,
(Am)   (D)
  And so I came to see him
      (Em)
And listen for a while.
(Am)   (D)
  And there he was, this young boy,
(G)   (B7)
  A stranger to my eyes.

© Copyright 1972 Fox-Gimbel Productions Incorporated, USA.
Assigned to Onward Music Limited, 11 Uxbridge Street, London W8
for the British Commonwealth (excluding Canada), Republics of South Africa and Eire.
All Rights Reserved. International Copyright Secured.

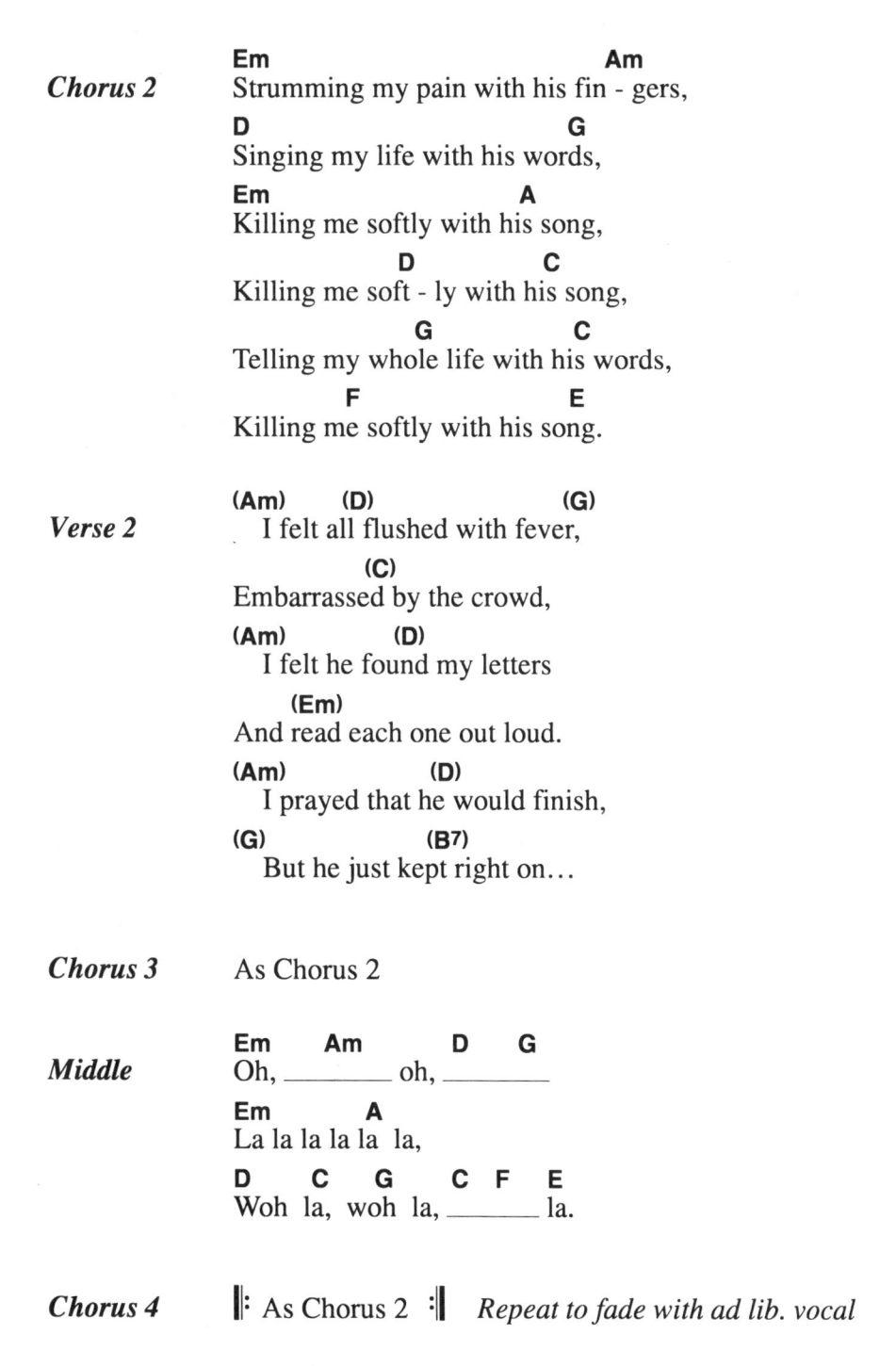

Chorus 2

```
       Em                              Am
       Strumming my pain with his fin - gers,
       D                          G
       Singing my life with his words,
       Em                   A
       Killing me softly with his song,
                       D        C
       Killing me soft - ly with his song,
                       G         C
       Telling my whole life with his words,
                 F            E
       Killing me softly with his song.
```

Verse 2

```
       (Am)    (D)              (G)
          I felt all flushed with fever,
                    (C)
       Embarrassed by the crowd,
       (Am)       (D)
          I felt he found my letters
             (Em)
       And read each one out loud.
       (Am)            (D)
          I prayed that he would finish,
       (G)              (B7)
          But he just kept right on…
```

Chorus 3   As Chorus 2

Middle

```
       Em     Am       D    G
       Oh, _____ oh, _____
       Em        A
       La la la la la  la,
       D    C    G    C  F    E
       Woh  la,  woh  la, _____ la.
```

Chorus 4   ‖: As Chorus 2 :‖   *Repeat to fade with ad lib. vocal*

Let Me Entertain You

Words & Music by
Guy Chambers & Robbie Williams

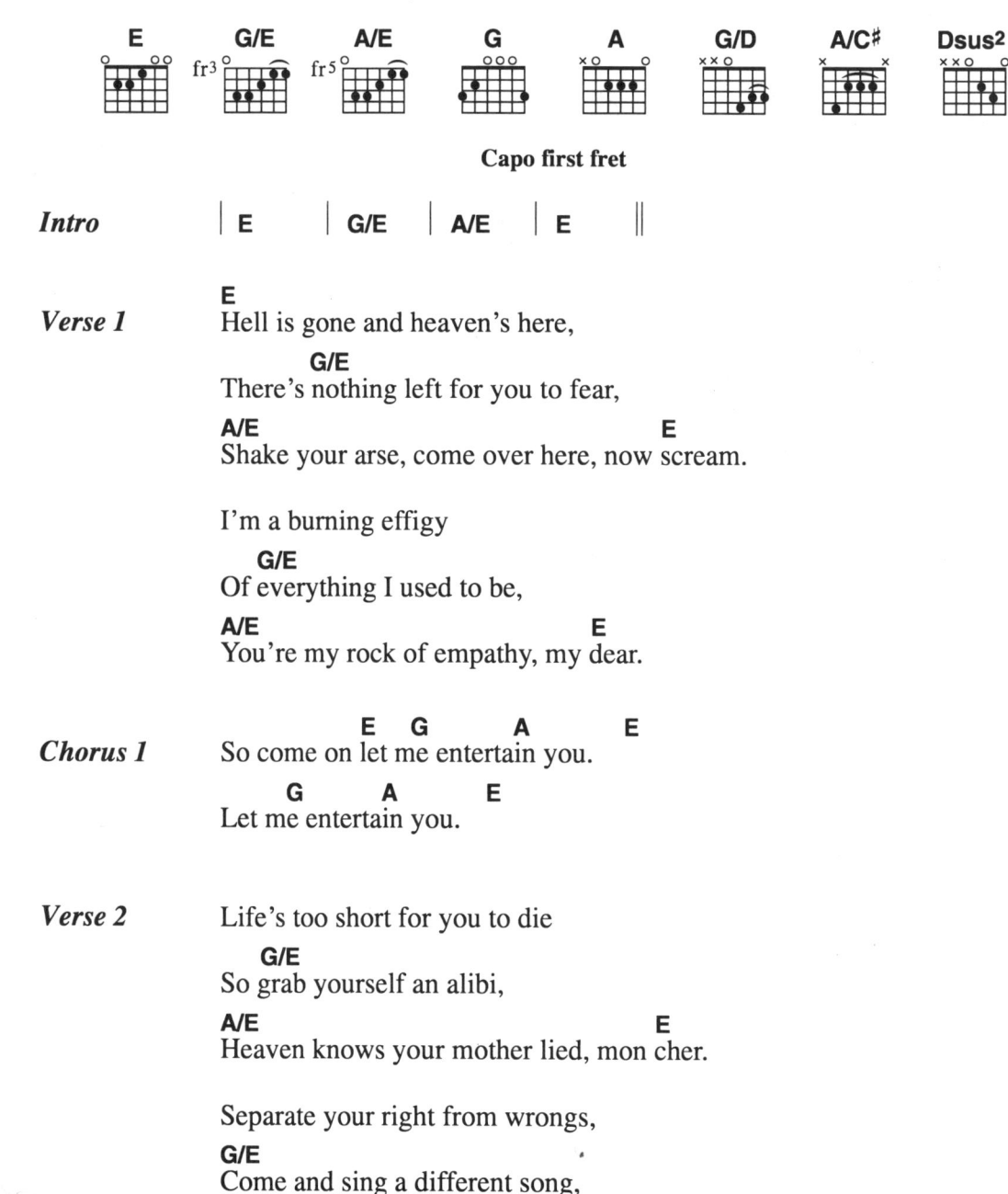

[Chord diagrams: E, G/E (fr3), A/E (fr5), G, A, G/D, A/C#, Dsus2]

Capo first fret

Intro | E | G/E | A/E | E ||

Verse 1
E
Hell is gone and heaven's here,
  G/E
There's nothing left for you to fear,
A/E   E
Shake your arse, come over here, now scream.

I'm a burning effigy
  G/E
Of everything I used to be,
A/E   E
You're my rock of empathy, my dear.

Chorus 1
             E G   A   E
So come on let me entertain you.
      G   A   E
Let me entertain you.

Verse 2
Life's too short for you to die
  G/E
So grab yourself an alibi,
A/E   E
Heaven knows your mother lied, mon cher.

Separate your right from wrongs,
G/E
Come and sing a different song,
    A/E   E
The kettle's on so don't be long, mon cher.

© Copyright 1997 EMI Virgin Music Limited, 127 Charing Cross Road, London WC2 (50%) &
BMG Music Publishing Limited, Bedford House, 69-79 Fulham High Street, London SW6 (50%).
This arrangement © 1999 BMG Music Publishing Limited for their share of interest.
All Rights Reserved. International Copyright Secured.

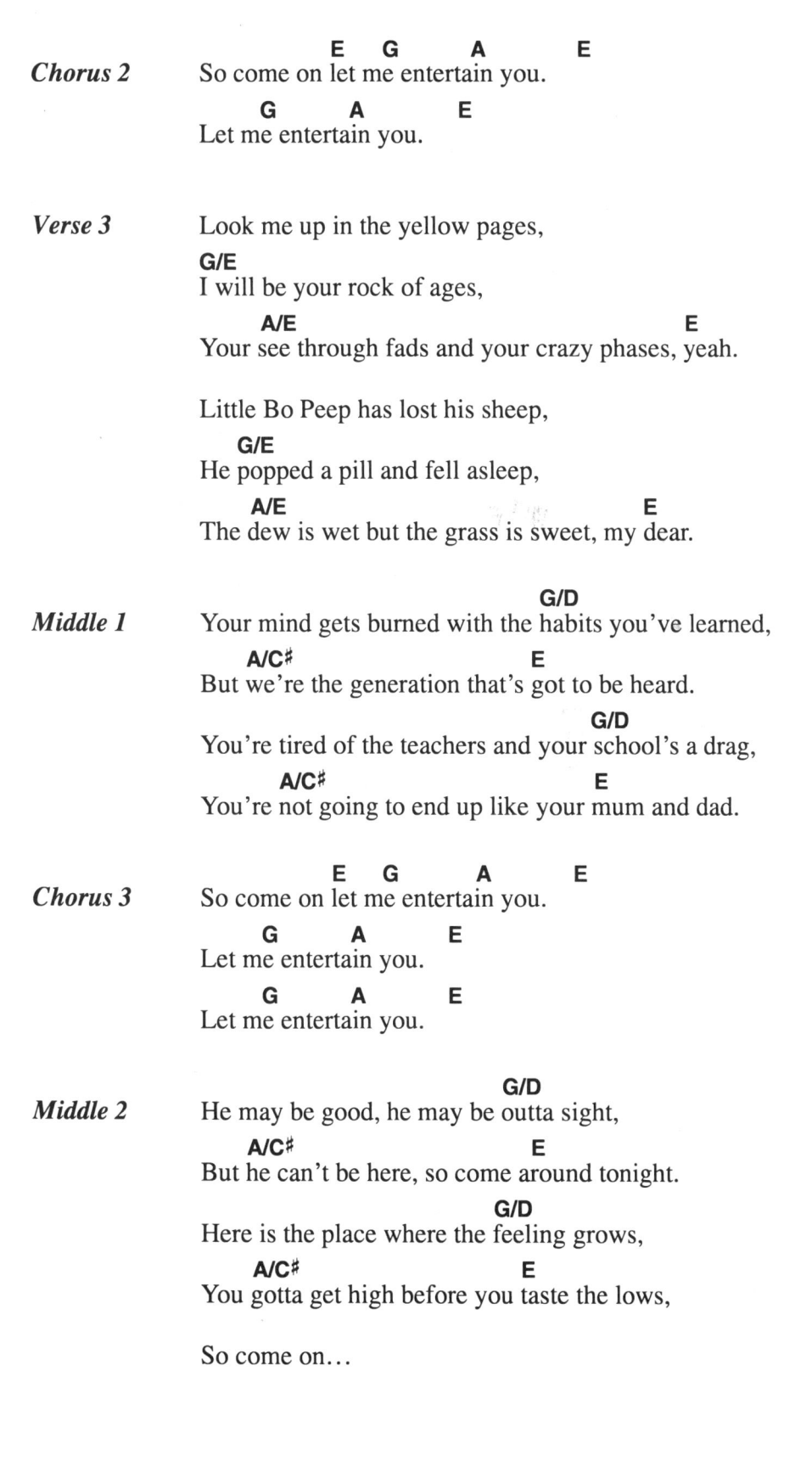

Chorus 2

     E G A   E
So come on let me entertain you.
    G A E
Let me entertain you.

Verse 3

Look me up in the yellow pages,
G/E
I will be your rock of ages,
  A/E   E
Your see through fads and your crazy phases, yeah.

Little Bo Peep has lost his sheep,
  G/E
He popped a pill and fell asleep,
 A/E   E
The dew is wet but the grass is sweet, my dear.

Middle 1

            G/D
Your mind gets burned with the habits you've learned,
  A/C♯   E
But we're the generation that's got to be heard.
          G/D
You're tired of the teachers and your school's a drag,
  A/C♯   E
You're not going to end up like your mum and dad.

Chorus 3

     E G A   E
So come on let me entertain you.
    G A E
Let me entertain you.
    G A E
Let me entertain you.

Middle 2

          G/D
He may be good, he may be outta sight,
  A/C♯   E
But he can't be here, so come around tonight.
         G/D
Here is the place where the feeling grows,
  A/C♯   E
You gotta get high before you taste the lows,

So come on…

Instrumental ‖: E | G/E | A/E | E   :‖

Chorus 4
```
           G     A      E
Let me entertain you,
           G     A      E
Let me entertain you,
           G     A      E
Let me entertain you,
           G     A      E
Let me entertain you.
```

Link   ‖: Come on, come on, come on, come on,
Dsus2
Come on, come on, come on, come on,
A/C#   E
Come on, come on, come on, come on.   :‖

Instrumental ‖: E | G | A | E   :‖

Outro
```
                    G
‖: Let me entertain you,
A           E
Let me entertain you.   :‖   Repeat to fade
```

Miami

Words & Music by Will Smith, Ryan Toby, Samuel Barnes,
Leon Sylvers III, Stephen Shockley & William Shelby

| B♭m | Fm7 | G♭maj7 | E♭m9 | Gm7♭5 |

Intro

B♭m   Fm7   G♭maj7   B♭m
  Uh!   Uh! Yeah, yeah, yeah, yeah, uh! Miami.

Fm7   G♭maj7   B♭m
  Uh! Uh! South Beach, bringin' in the heat. Uh!

Fm7   G♭maj7
  Ha, ha, can y'all feel that?
                              B♭m
Can y'all feel that?

Fm7   G♭maj7
  Jig it out, uh.

Verse 1

      B♭m   Fm7
Here I am in the place where I come, let go.
              G♭maj7
In Miami, the bass and the sun set low.
      B♭m   Fm7
Ev'ry day like a Mardi Gras, ev'rybody party all day,
       G♭maj7
No work, all play O.K.
      B♭m   Fm7
So we sip a little somethin' later as a spell,
                     G♭maj7
Me and Charlie at the bar runnin' up a high bill.
        B♭m   Fm7
Nothin' less than ill, when we dress to kill,
                    G♭maj7
Ev'ry time the ladies pass they be like "Hi Will."

Verse 2

          B♭m   Fm7
Can y'all feel me? All ages and races,
              G♭maj7
Real sweet faces, every diff'rent nation.
     B♭m   Fm7   G♭maj7
Spanish, Haitian, Indian, Jamaican, black, white, Cuban and Asian.

© Copyright 1998 Treyball Music, Pladid Music, Slam U Well & Spectrum VII, USA.
Notting Hill Music (UK) Limited, 8B Berkeley Gardens, London W8 (30%), Warner Chappell Music Limited,
Griffin House, 161 Hammersmith Road, London W6 (10%), Sony/ATV Music Publishing (UK) Limited,
10 Great Marlborough Street, London W1 (50%) & Copyright Control (10%).
All Rights Reserved. International Copyright Secured.

cont.

        E♭m9
I only came for two days of playin',

But ev'ry time I always wind up stayin'.

This is the type of town I could spend a few days in.
                             Gm7♭5
Miami, the city that keeps the roof blazin'.

Chorus 1

  B♭m   **Fm7**
Party in the city where the heat is on,
             G♭maj7
All night on the beach to the break of dawn.
B♭m   **Fm7**   **G♭maj7**
"Welcome to Miami, bienvenida a Miami."
B♭m   **Fm7**
Bouncin' in the club when the heat is on,
             G♭maj7
All night on the beach to the break of dawn.
   B♭m   **Fm7**   **G♭maj7**
I'm goin' to Miami. "Welcome to Miami."

Verse 3

       E♭m9
Yo, I heard the rainstorms ain't nothin' to mess with,

But I can't feel a drip on the strip, it's a trip.

Ladies half dressed, fully equipped,
                             Gm7♭5
And they be screamin' out, "Will, we loved your last hit."
N.C.   **B♭m**   **Fm7**
So I'm thinkin' I'm a scoop, me somethin' hot (hot hot),
             G♭maj7
And this Salsa Meringue meltin' pot.
  B♭m   **Fm7**
Hottest club in the city and it's right on the beach,

Temperature get to you.

Verse 4

G♭maj7   **B♭m**   **Fm7**
It's about to reach five hundred degrees in the Caribbean Seas,
          G♭maj7
With the hot mommies screamin', "Ah, Poppy!"
  B♭m   **Fm7**
Every time I come to town, they be spottin' me,
             G♭maj7
In the drop Bentley, ain't no stoppin' me.
  B♭m   **Fm7**
So cash in your dough and flow to this fashion show,

cont.

                       G♭maj7
Pound for pound, anywhere you go.

    B♭m   **Fm7**
Yo, ain't no city in the world like this, (uh-huh, uh-huh,)

                                G♭maj7
And if you ask how I know, I gots ta plead the fifth, Miami.

Chorus 2   As Chorus 1

Verse 5

          B♭m   **Fm7**
Don't get me wrong, Chi'town got it goin' on,

                   G♭maj7
And New York is the city that we know don't sleep.

      B♭m   **Fm7**
And we all know that L A and Philly stay jiggy,

          G♭maj7   **B♭m**
But on the sneak Miami bringin' heat (for real).

      Fm7
Y'all don't understand,

                          G♭maj7
I've never seen so many Dominican women with cinnamon tans.

B♭m   **Fm7**
  Mira, this is the plan,

                        G♭maj7
Take a walk on the beach, draw a heart in the sand.

Verse 6

              B♭m
Gimme ya hand, damn, you look sexy (woo),

Fm7   **G♭maj7**
  Let's go to my yacht in the West Keys.

            B♭m
Ride my jet-skis, loungin' under the palm trees,

Fm7   **G♭maj7**
  'Cos ya gotta have cheese for the Summer House piece on South Beach.

E♭m9
Water so clear, you can see to the bottom,

Hundred thousand dollar cars, everybody got 'em.

Ain't no surprise in the club to see Sly Stallone,

          Gm7♭5
Miami, my second home, Miami.

Chorus 3 & 4   ‖: As Chorus 1 :‖

      N.C.
Party in the city where the heat is on.

One For Sorrow

Words & Music by
Topham/Twigg/Ellington

Intro
| A♭ | A♭ | E♭/G | E♭/G | B♭m/F | B♭m/F | E♭sus⁴ | E♭ ||

Verse 1
      A♭   E♭/G
I wanted your love but look what it's done to me,
    B♭m/F
All my dreams have come to nothing.
E♭sus⁴   E♭
Who would have believed
    A♭   E♭/G
All the laughter that we shared would be a memory.
B♭m/F
I cannot count the tears you've caused me,
E♭sus⁴   E♭
If I could have seen,
     D♭   A♭/C   D♭m/F♭   E♭11
And do you ever think of me and how we used to be?

Chorus 1
    A♭   Caug
Oh, I know you're somewhere else right now
  Fm   F/A
And loving someone else, no doubt.
     B♭m   B♭m/A♭   E♭7
Well, I'm one for sorrow, ain't it too, too bad?
   A♭   Caug
Are you breaking someone else's heart
    Fm   F/A
'Cos you're taking my love where you are?
   B♭m   B♭m/A♭   E♭7   A♭
Well, I'm one for sorrow, ain't it too, too bad about us?

© Copyright 1998 All Boys Music Limited, 4-7 The Vineyard, Sanctuary Street, London SE1 1QL.
All Rights Reserved. International Copyright Secured.

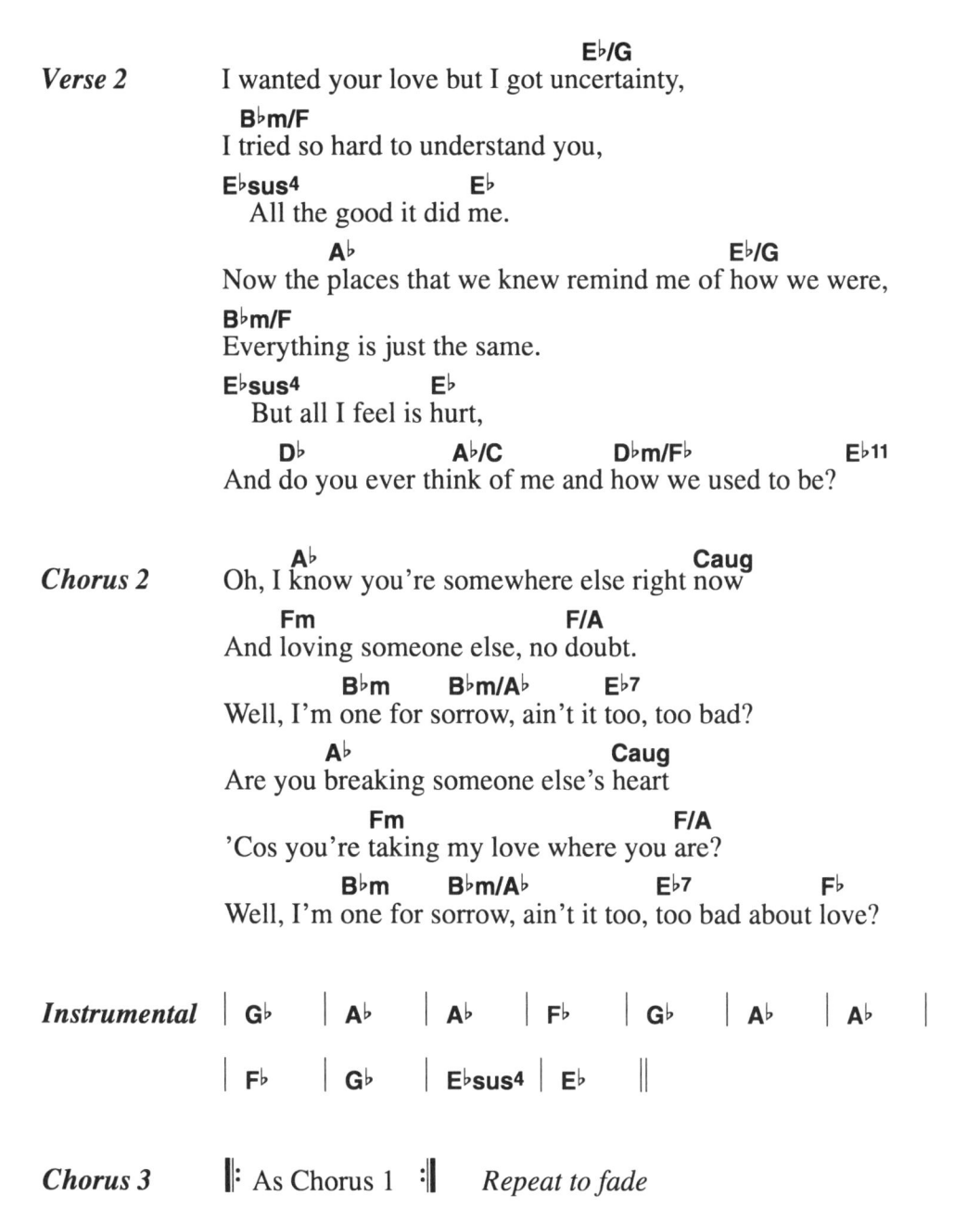

Verse 2

                                                          E♭/G
I wanted your love but I got uncertainty,
  B♭m/F
I tried so hard to understand you,
E♭sus4   **E♭**
  All the good it did me.
        A♭   **E♭/G**
Now the places that we knew remind me of how we were,
B♭m/F
Everything is just the same.
E♭sus4   **E♭**
  But all I feel is hurt,
     D♭   **A♭/C**   **D♭m/F♭**   **E♭11**
And do you ever think of me and how we used to be?

Chorus 2

      A♭   **Caug**
Oh, I know you're somewhere else right now
   Fm   **F/A**
And loving someone else, no doubt.
        B♭m **B♭m/A♭**   **E♭7**
Well, I'm one for sorrow, ain't it too, too bad?
    A♭   **Caug**
Are you breaking someone else's heart
     Fm   **F/A**
'Cos you're taking my love where you are?
       B♭m **B♭m/A♭**   **E♭7**   **F♭**
Well, I'm one for sorrow, ain't it too, too bad about love?

Instrumental | G♭ | A♭ | A♭ | F♭ | G♭ | A♭ | A♭ |

                         | F♭ | G♭ | E♭sus4 | E♭ ||

Chorus 3 ||: As Chorus 1 :|| *Repeat to fade*

Thank U

Words by Alanis Morissette
Music by Alanis Morissette & Glenn Ballard

Cmaj7   G   Fadd2   F   F/G

Intro | Cmaj7 | Cmaj7 | G | Fadd2 ||

Verse 1
Cmaj7   G   Fadd2
How 'bout getting off o' these antibio - tics?
Cmaj7   G   Fadd2
How 'bout stopping eating when I'm full up?
Cmaj7   G   Fadd2
How 'bout them transparent dangling carrots?
Cmaj7   G   Fadd2
How 'bout that ever elusive ku - do?

Chorus 1
              Cmaj7
Thank you India, thank you terror;
              G   F
Thank you dis - illusionment.
         F/G   Cmaj7
Thank you frailty, thank you consequence;
              G   F
Thank you, thank you silence.

Verse 2
Cmaj7   G   Fadd2
How 'bout me not blaming you for ev'ry - thing?
Cmaj7   G   Fadd2
How 'bout me enjoying the moment for once?
Cmaj7   G   Fadd2
How 'bout how good it feels to fin'lly forgive you?
Cmaj7   G   Fadd2
How 'bout grieving it all one at a time?

Chorus 2   As Chorus 1

© Copyright 1998 Aerostation Corporation & 1974 Music, USA.
MCA Music Limited, 77 Fulham Palace Road, London W6.
All Rights Reserved. International Copyright Secured.

Middle

     Cmaj7
The moment I let go of it
       G   **F**   **F/G**
Was the mo - ment I got more than I⎵ could handle.
     Cmaj7
The moment I jumped off of it
       G   **F**
Was the mo - ment I touched down.

Verse 3

Cmaj7   **G**   **Fadd2**
How 'bout no longer being masochis - tic?
Cmaj7   **G**   **Fadd2**
How 'bout remembering your divinity?
Cmaj7   **G**   **Fadd2**
How 'bout unabashedly bawling your eyes out?
Cmaj7   **G**   **Fadd2**
How 'bout not equating death with stopping?

Chorus 3

           Cmaj7
Thank you India, thank you providence;
        G   **F**
Thank you dis - illusionment.
      F/G   **Cmaj7**
Thank you no - thingness, thank you clarity;
       G   **F**
Thank you, thank you silence.

Ad lib. vocal to fade

This Is Hardcore

Lyrics by Jarvis Cocker. Music by Jarvis Cocker, Nick Banks,
Candida Doyle, Steve Mackey, Mark Webber & Peter Thomas

Intro ‖: Gmaj7 | Gmaj7 | Gmaj7 | Gmaj7 :‖ *Play 3 times*

| Em9 | Gmaj7/D♯ | Gmaj7/D | Gmaj7/C♯ | Em | B/D♯ |

| G/D | A | Em9 | Em9 | Em9 | Em9 ‖

Verse 1

Gmaj7
You are hardcore, you make me hard,

Em9　　　　　　　　　Gmaj7/F♯
You name the drama and I'll play the part.

Em9　　　　　　　　　Gmaj7
It seems I saw you in some teenage wet dream,

Em9　　　　　　　　　Gmaj7/F♯
I like your get up if you know what I mean.

Em9　　　Gmaj7/D♯　Gmaj7/D　　　Gmaj7/C♯
I want it bad,　　　　　　I want it now.

Em9　　　　　B/D♯　G/D　　　　A
Oh can't you see　　I'm ready now?

Em9　　　　　　　　　　Gmaj7/D♯
I've seen all the pictures, I studied them for ever.

Gmaj7/D　　　　　　　Gmaj7/C♯
I wanna make a movie so let's star in it together, oh,

(C)　　　　　　(G)　　　Em9
Don't make a move 'til I say "action".

(C)　　　　　　　　　Em9
Oh here comes the hardcore life.

© Copyright 1998 Island Music Limited, 47 British Grove, London W4 & Ring Musik GmbH.
All Rights Reserved. International Copyright Secured.

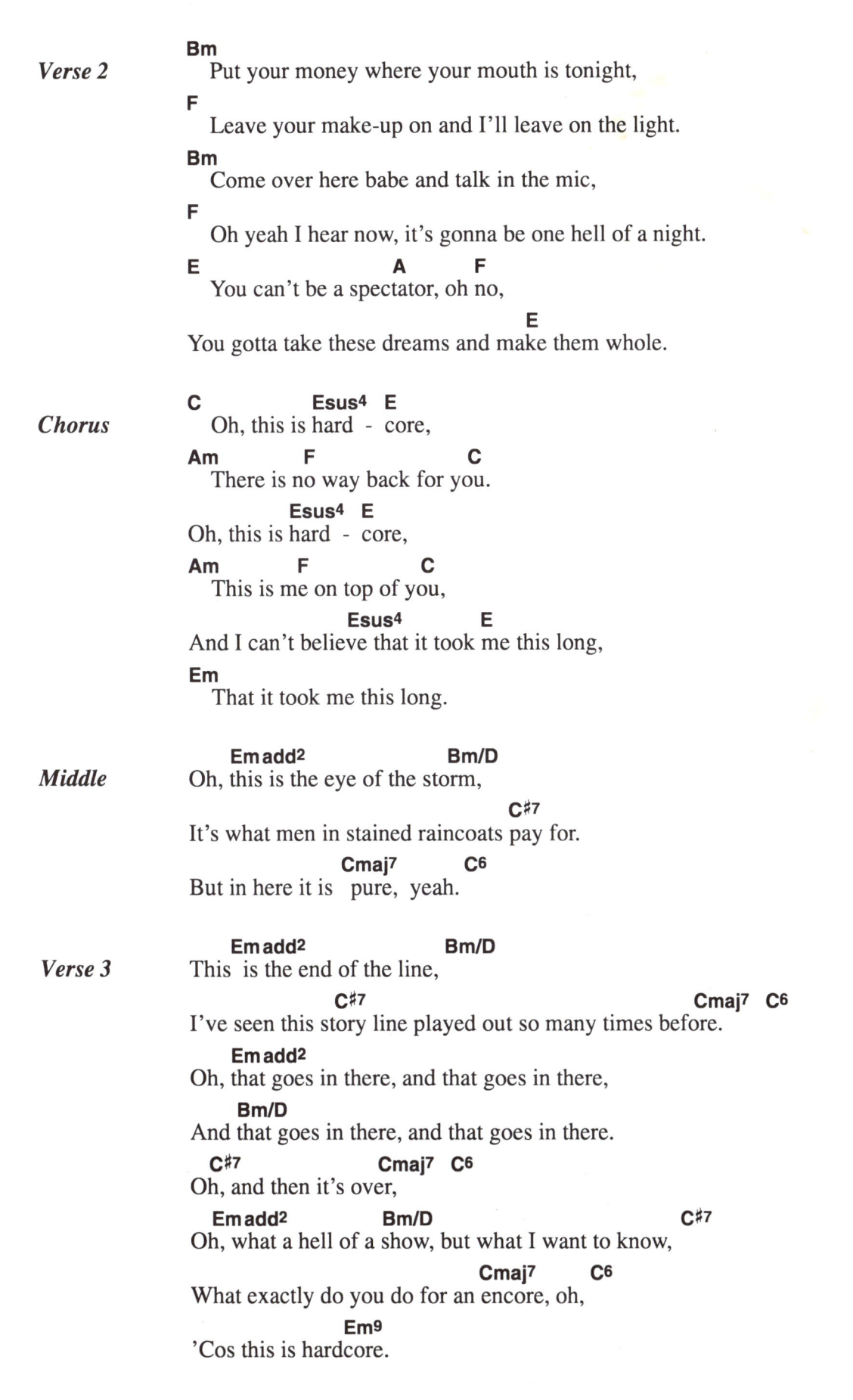

Verse 2

    Bm
    Put your money where your mouth is tonight,
    F
    Leave your make-up on and I'll leave on the light.
    Bm
    Come over here babe and talk in the mic,
    F
    Oh yeah I hear now, it's gonna be one hell of a night.
E   **A**   **F**
You can't be a spectator, oh no,
                                      E
You gotta take these dreams and make them whole.

Chorus

  C   **Esus⁴ E**
  Oh, this is hard - core,
Am   **F**   **C**
There is no way back for you.
         Esus⁴ E
Oh, this is hard - core,
Am   **F**   **C**
This is me on top of you,
        Esus⁴   **E**
And I can't believe that it took me this long,
Em
That it took me this long.

Middle

  Em add²   **Bm/D**
Oh, this is the eye of the storm,
                        C♯7
It's what men in stained raincoats pay for.
                Cmaj⁷   **C⁶**
But in here it is pure, yeah.

Verse 3

  Em add²   **Bm/D**
This is the end of the line,
      C♯7   **Cmaj⁷ C⁶**
I've seen this story line played out so many times before.
  Em add²
Oh, that goes in there, and that goes in there,
  Bm/D
And that goes in there, and that goes in there.
  C♯7   **Cmaj⁷ C⁶**
Oh, and then it's over,
  Em add²   **Bm/D**   **C♯7**
Oh, what a hell of a show, but what I want to know,
                      Cmaj⁷   **C⁶**
What exactly do you do for an encore, oh,
            Em⁹
'Cos this is hardcore.

Torn

Words & Music by
Anne Preven, Scott Cutler & Phil Thornalley

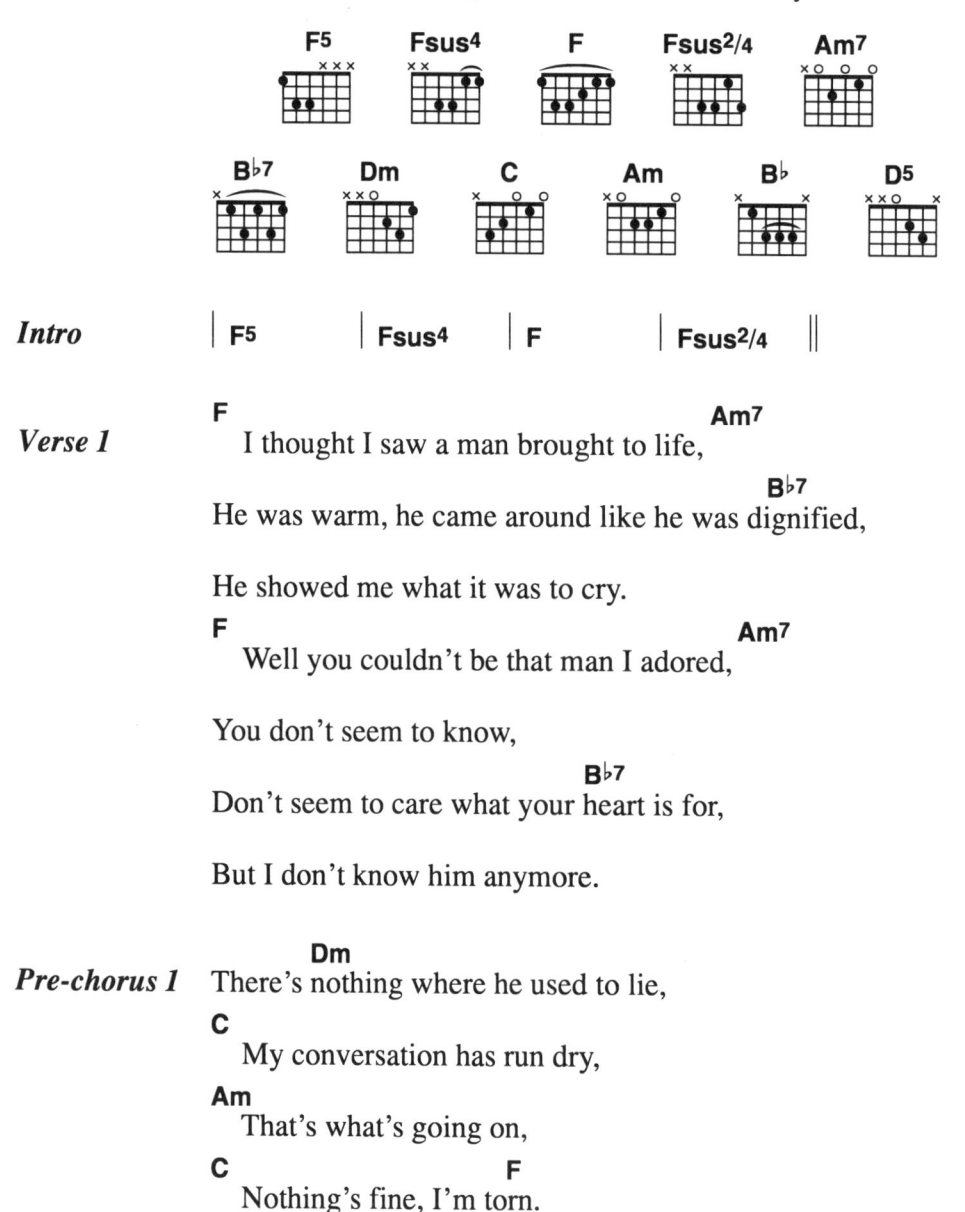

Intro | F5 | Fsus4 | F | Fsus2/4 ||

Verse 1
    F   Am7
I thought I saw a man brought to life,
                                    Bb7
He was warm, he came around like he was dignified,

He showed me what it was to cry.
   F   Am7
Well you couldn't be that man I adored,

You don't seem to know,
                     Bb7
Don't seem to care what your heart is for,

But I don't know him anymore.

Pre-chorus 1
        Dm
There's nothing where he used to lie,
C
  My conversation has run dry,
Am
  That's what's going on,
C   F
  Nothing's fine, I'm torn.

© Copyright 1997 BMG Music Publishing Limited, Bedford House, 69-79 Fulham High Street,
London SW6 (33.33%), Weetie Pie Music/Island Music Limited, 47 British Grove, London W4 (33.33%) &
Scott Cutler Music/Screen Gems-EMI Music Limited, 127 Charing Cross Road, London WC2 (33.34%).
This arrangement © 1999 BMG Music Publishing Limited for their share of interest.
All Rights Reserved. International Copyright Secured.

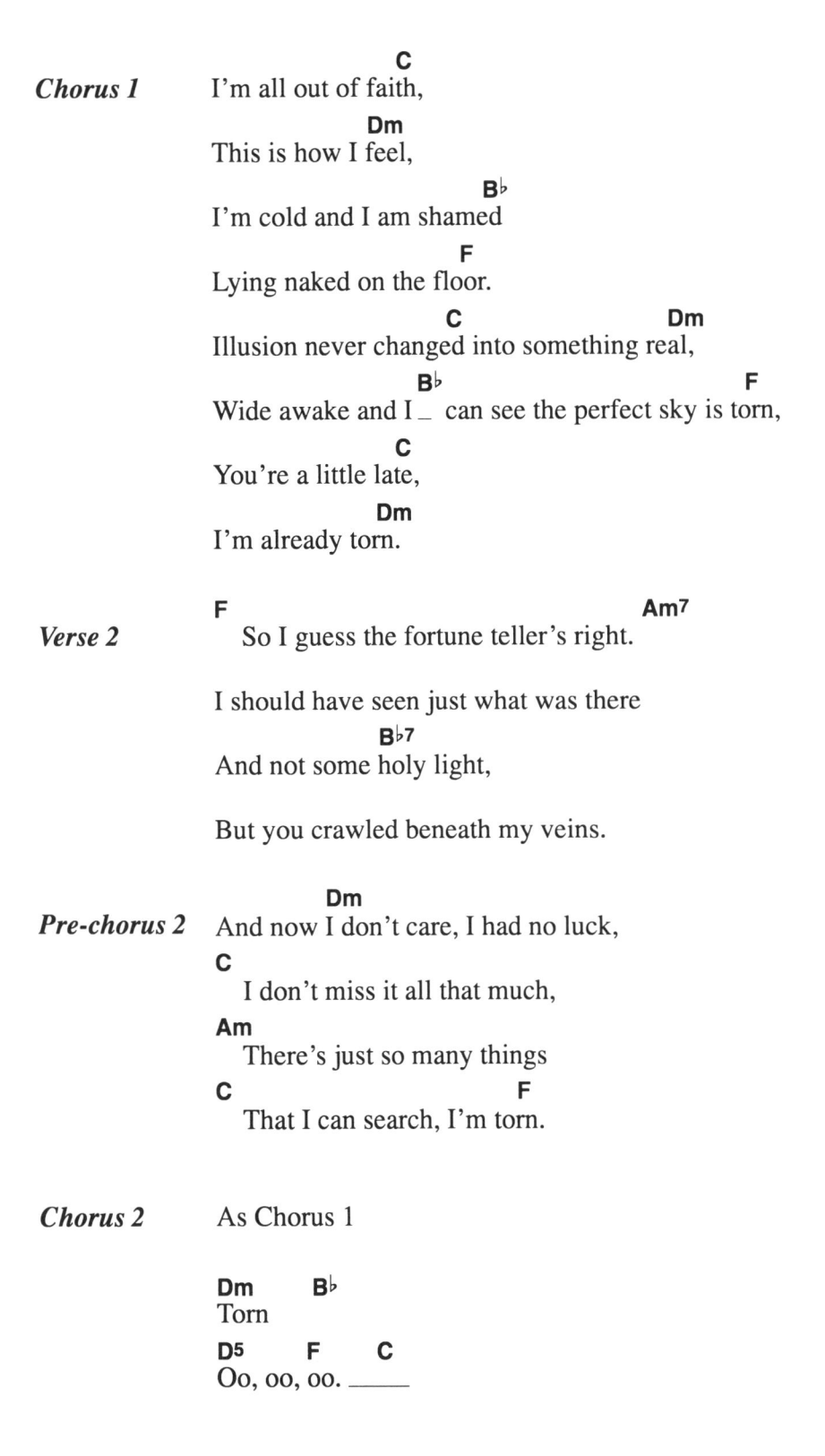

Chorus 1

        C
I'm all out of faith,
              Dm
This is how I feel,
                  B♭
I'm cold and I am shamed
               F
Lying naked on the floor.
                    C   **Dm**
Illusion never changed into something real,
          B♭   **F**
Wide awake and I _ can see the perfect sky is torn,
         C
You're a little late,
       Dm
I'm already torn.

Verse 2

   F   **Am7**
    So I guess the fortune teller's right.

I should have seen just what was there
             B♭7
And not some holy light,

But you crawled beneath my veins.

Pre-chorus 2

           Dm
And now I don't care, I had no luck,
C
  I don't miss it all that much,
Am
  There's just so many things
C   **F**
  That I can search, I'm torn.

Chorus 2   As Chorus 1

Dm   **B♭**
Torn
D5   **F**   **C**
Oo, oo, oo. _____

Pre-chorus 3
        Dm
There's nothing where he used to lie,
  C
    My inspiration has run dry,
Am
    That's what's going on,
C   **F**
    Nothing's right, I'm torn.

Chorus 3
            C
I'm all out of faith,
         Dm
This is how I feel,
                 B♭
I'm cold and I am shamed,
             F
Lying naked on the floor.
                C   **Dm**
Illusion never changed into something real,
        B♭   **F**
Wide awake and I _ can see the perfect sky is torn.

Chorus 4
            C
I'm all out of faith,
         Dm
This is how I feel,
                 B♭
I'm cold and I'm ashamed,
                 F
Bound and broken on the floor.
           C
You're a little late,
            Dm **B♭**
I'm already torn…
Dm   **C**
Torn…

Repeat Chorus ad lib. to fade

Until The Time Is Through

Words & Music by
Max Martin & Andreas Carlsson

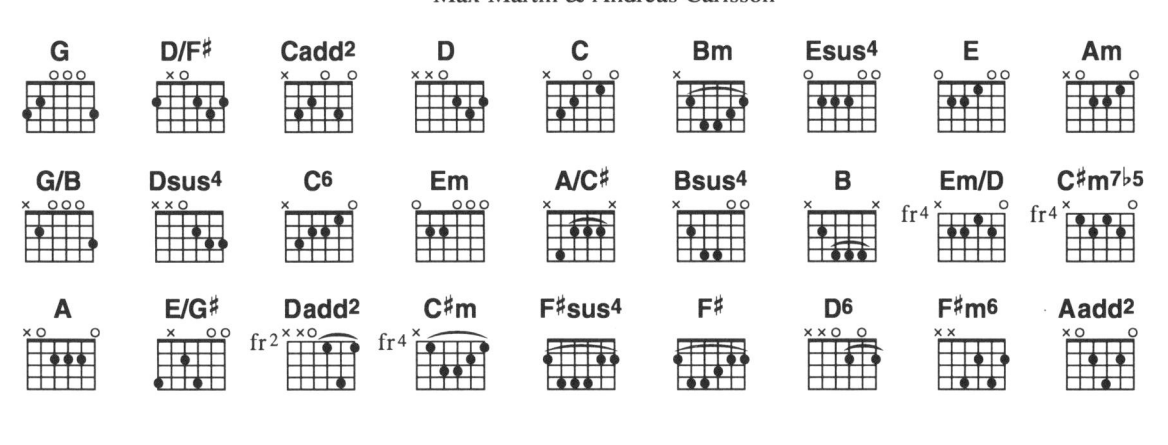

[Chord diagrams: G, D/F#, Cadd2, D, C, Bm, Esus4, E, Am, G/B, Dsus4, C6, Em, A/C#, Bsus4, B, Em/D, C#m7♭5, A, E/G#, Dadd2, C#m, F#sus4, F#, D6, F#m6, Aadd2]

Intro
     G   D/F# Cadd2   D
Now and forever, until the time is through.

Verse 1
G
I can't believe it,

D/F#   C   D
Don't know where to start, no ba-by.

G
So many questions

D/F#   C   D
Deep inside my heart, you know that.

Bm   Esus4   E
Give me a moment before you go,

           Am   G/B   C   D
There's something you ought to know.

Chorus 1
       G
Baby, now and forever

D/F#   Cadd2
Until the time is through,

   D
I'll be standing here

G   D/F#   Cadd2
Waiting, and never give up my faith in you,

      D
Trying to make it clear.

© Copyright 1998 Grantsville Publishing Limited administered by
Zomba Music Publishers Limited, 165-167 High Road, London NW10.
All Rights Reserved. International Copyright Secured.

cont.

     Bm   **Esus4** **E**
Without your love I'll be half   a man,

  Am   **G/B**   **Dsus4** **D**
Maybe one day you will un - der - stand.

G
Now and forever

C6   **D**   **G**   **D/F#**
Until the time is through,

        Cadd2   **D**
I'll be waiting.

Verse 2

G
How can I tell you

D/F#   **C**
So that you can see?

   D   **G**
You know that life has a meaning

    D/F#   **C**
When you are here with me.

          D
(When you are here with me, baby.)

Bm   **Esus4** **E**
Give me a moment before you go,

     Am   **G/B**   **C**   **D**
There's something you ought to know.

Chorus 2

      G
Baby, now and forever

D/F#   **Cadd2**
Until the time is through,

  D
I'll be standing here

G   **D/F#**   **Cadd2**
Waiting, and never give up my faith in you,

    D
Trying to make it clear.

Bm   **Esus4** **E**
Without your love I'll be half   a man,

  Am   **G/B**   **Dsus4** **D**
Maybe one day you will un - der - stand.

G
Now and forever

C6   **D**   **Em**
Until the time is through.

Middle

        A/C#   D
There is no one to comfort me
                Bsus4   B   Em
Here in my cold   real - ity. —
             Em/D
I'm searching for words,
         C#m7♭5   D
What can I say to make you see?

| G | D | Cadd2 | (Dsus4) (D) ||

      A   E/G#   Dadd2   E
Baby now until time is through, I'll be here.
      A   E/G#   Dadd2   E
Baby now until time is through, I'll be here.

Chorus 3

     A
Baby, now and forever
E/G#   Dadd2
Until the time is through,
    E
I'll be standing here
A   E/G#   Dadd2
Waiting, and never give up my faith in you,
    E
Trying to make it clear.
C#m   F#sus4 F#
Without your love I'll be half a   man,
Bm   A/C#   Esus4 D
Maybe one day you will un - der - stand.
A
Now and forever
D6   E   F#m6
I will be here for you,
D   E   Aadd2
Until the time is through.

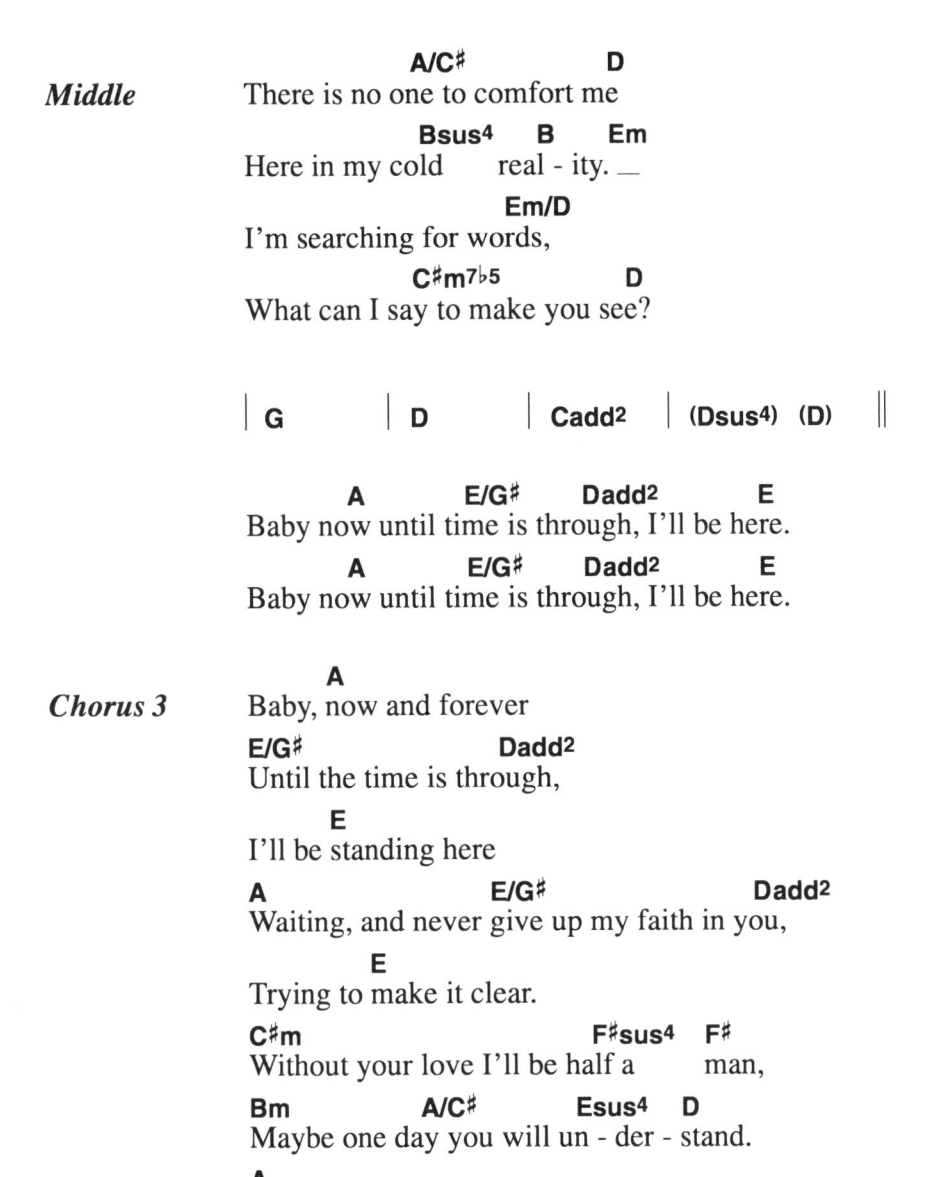

You Don't Care About Us

Words & Music by
Placebo

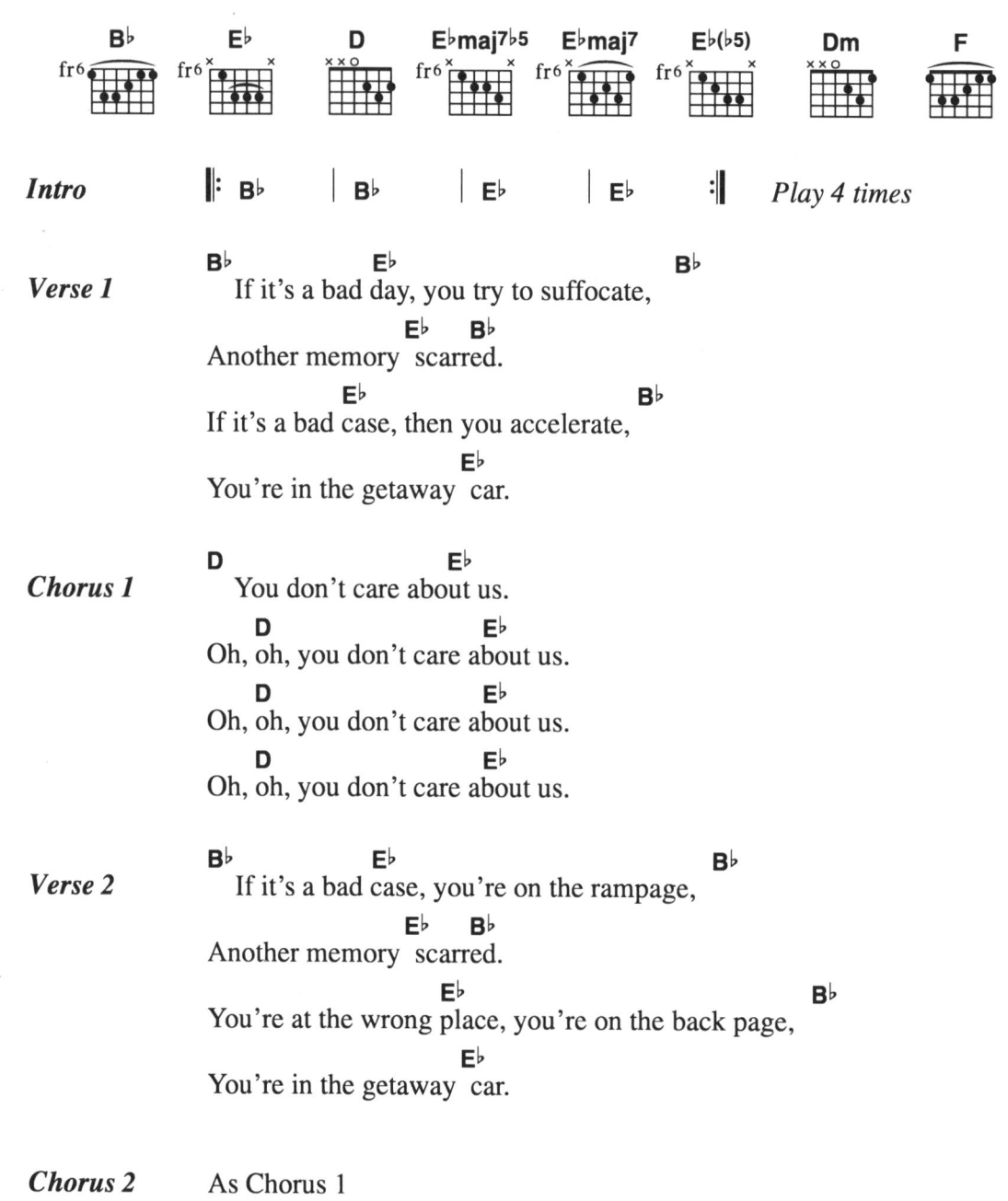

[Chord diagrams: B♭, E♭, D, E♭maj7♭5, E♭maj7, E♭(♭5), Dm, F]

Intro   ‖: B♭ | B♭ | E♭ | E♭ :‖   Play 4 times

Verse 1
    B♭   E♭   B♭
If it's a bad day, you try to suffocate,
                  E♭   B♭
Another memory scarred.
           E♭   B♭
If it's a bad case, then you accelerate,
                  E♭
You're in the getaway car.

Chorus 1
    D   E♭
You don't care about us.
        D   E♭
Oh, oh, you don't care about us.
        D   E♭
Oh, oh, you don't care about us.
        D   E♭
Oh, oh, you don't care about us.

Verse 2
    B♭   E♭   B♭
If it's a bad case, you're on the rampage,
                  E♭   B♭
Another memory scarred.
                  E♭   B♭
You're at the wrong place, you're on the back page,
                  E♭
You're in the getaway car.

Chorus 2   As Chorus 1

© Copyright 1998 Famous Music Corporation, USA.
All Rights Reserved. International Copyright Secured.

Middle
    E♭maj7♭5 E♭   E♭maj7 E♭(♭5)
         It's your age.   It's my rage.

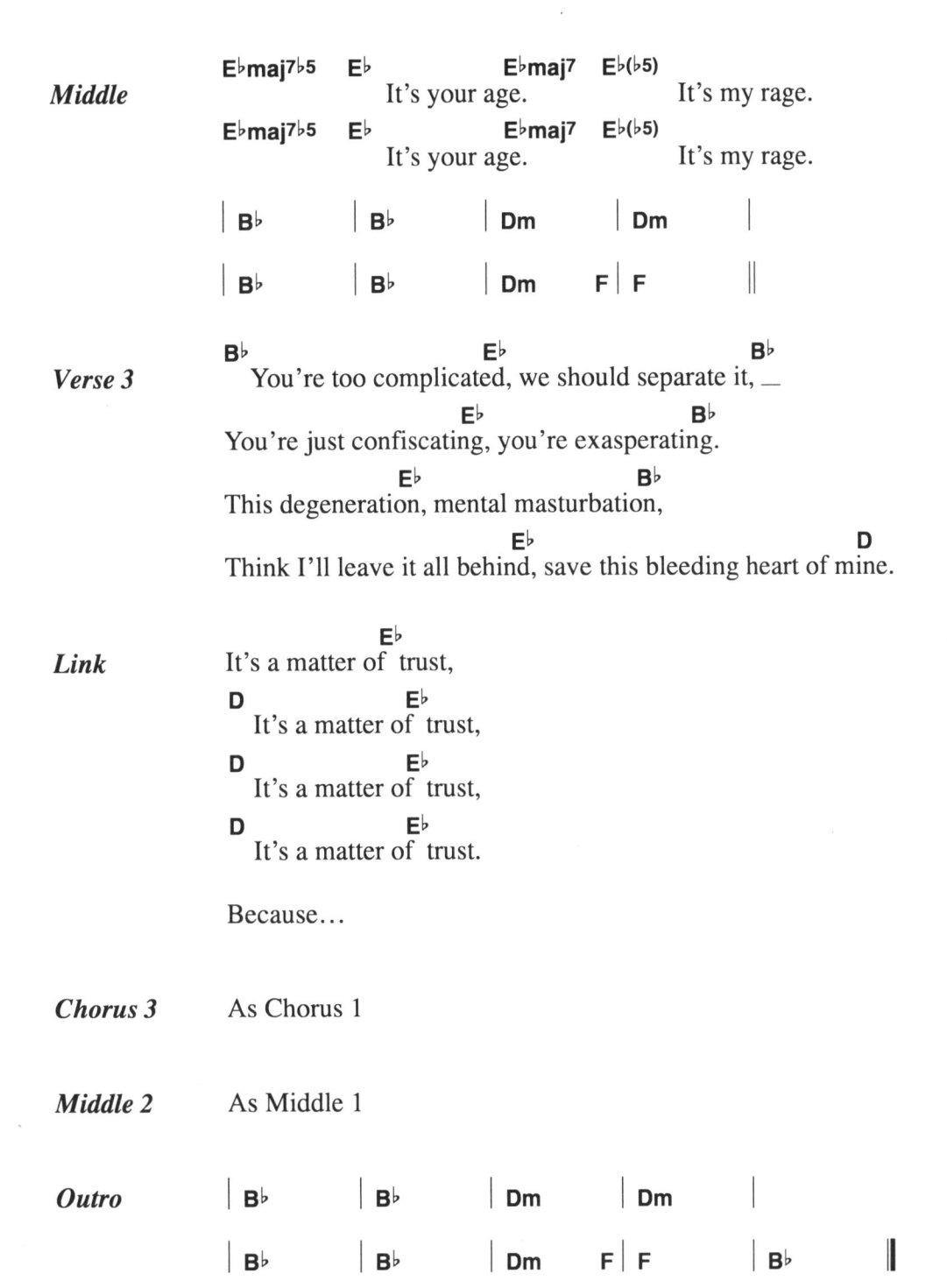

    E♭maj7♭5 E♭   E♭maj7 E♭(♭5)
         It's your age.   It's my rage.

| B♭ | B♭ | Dm | Dm | |
| B♭ | B♭ | Dm | F F | |

Verse 3
  B♭   E♭   B♭
    You're too complicated, we should separate it, —
               E♭   B♭
You're just confiscating, you're exasperating.
          E♭   B♭
This degeneration, mental masturbation,
               E♭   D
Think I'll leave it all behind, save this bleeding heart of mine.

Link
          E♭
It's a matter of trust,
D   E♭
  It's a matter of trust,
D   E♭
  It's a matter of trust,
D   E♭
  It's a matter of trust.

Because…

Chorus 3   As Chorus 1

Middle 2   As Middle 1

Outro
| B♭ | B♭ | Dm | Dm | | |
| B♭ | B♭ | Dm | F F | B♭ | |

Stop

Words & Music by Victoria Aadams, Emma Bunton, Melanie Brown,
Melanie Chisholm, Geri Halliwell, Andy Watkins & Paul Wilson

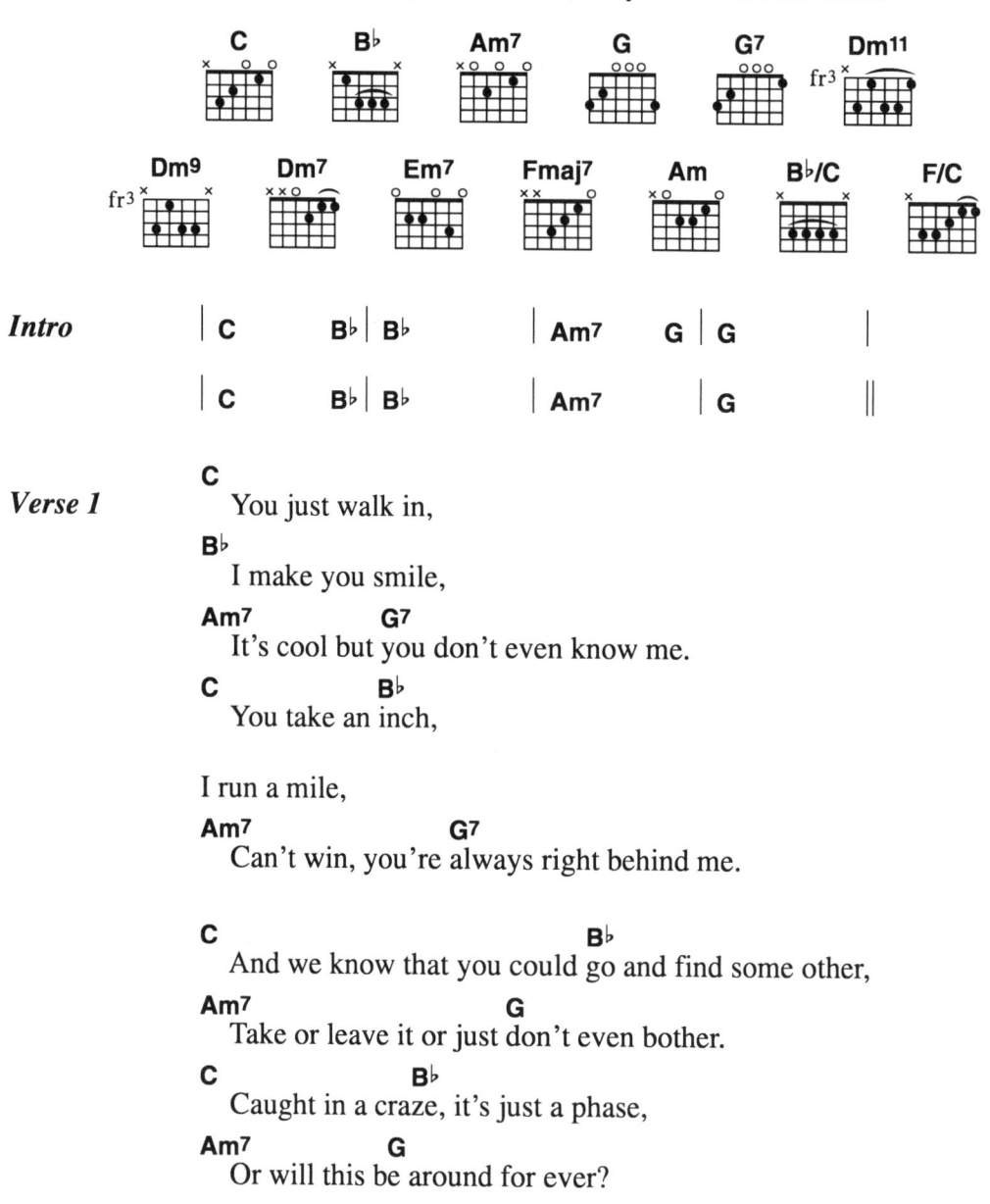

Intro | C   B♭ | B♭ | Am7   G | G |
             | C   B♭ | B♭ | Am7 | G ||

Verse 1
C
You just walk in,
B♭
I make you smile,
Am7   G7
It's cool but you don't even know me.
C   B♭
You take an inch,

I run a mile,
Am7   G7
Can't win, you're always right behind me.

C   B♭
And we know that you could go and find some other,
Am7   G
Take or leave it or just don't even bother.
C   B♭
Caught in a craze, it's just a phase,
Am7   G
Or will this be around for ever?

© Copyright 1997 Windswept Pacific Music Limited, Hope House, 40 St Peter's Road, London W6 (50%) &
19 Music/BMG Music Publishing Limited, Bedford House, 69-79 Fulham High Street, London SW6 (50%).
This arrangement © Copyright 1999 BMG Music Publishing Limited for their share of interest.
All Rights Reserved. International Copyright Secured.

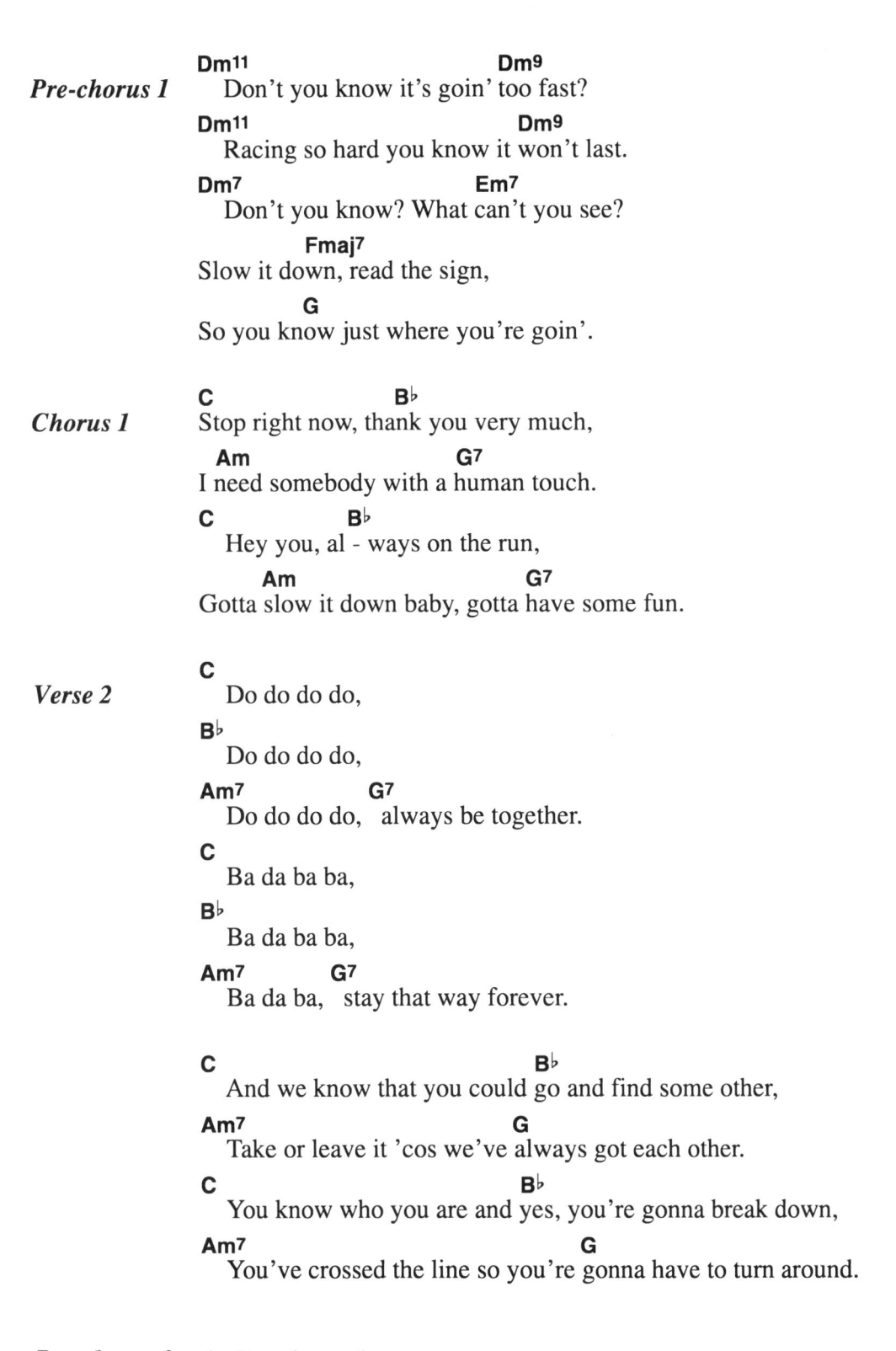

Pre-chorus 1

     Dm11   **Dm9**
Don't you know it's goin' too fast?
  Dm11   **Dm9**
Racing so hard you know it won't last.
  Dm7   **Em7**
Don't you know? What can't you see?
        Fmaj7
Slow it down, read the sign,
     G
So you know just where you're goin'.

Chorus 1

 C   **B♭**
Stop right now, thank you very much,
 Am   **G7**
I need somebody with a human touch.
 C   **B♭**
  Hey you, al - ways on the run,
   Am   **G7**
Gotta slow it down baby, gotta have some fun.

Verse 2

 C
  Do do do do,
B♭
  Do do do do,
Am7   **G7**
  Do do do do,   always be together.
C
  Ba da ba ba,
B♭
  Ba da ba ba,
Am7   **G7**
  Ba da ba,   stay that way forever.

 C   **B♭**
  And we know that you could go and find some other,
Am7   **G**
Take or leave it 'cos we've always got each other.
 C   **B♭**
  You know who you are and yes, you're gonna break down,
Am7   **G**
  You've crossed the line so you're gonna have to turn around.

Pre-chorus 2   As Pre-chorus 1

Chorus 2   As Chorus 1

Middle | (C) | (C) | (C) | (C) ||

        C
Gotta keep it down honey,
              Bb/C
Lay your back on the line,
                F/C
'Cos I don't care about the money,
          Bb/C
Don't be wastin' my time.

         C
You need less speed,
Bb/C
Get off my case,
            F/C
You gotta slow it down baby,
         G
Just get out of my face.

Chorus 3
       C   Bb
Stop right now, thank you very much,
    Am   G7
I need somebody with a human touch.
    C   Bb
    Hey you, al - ways on the run,
        Am   G7
Gotta slow it down baby, gotta have some fun.

Chorus 4
       C   Bb
Stop right now, thank you very much,
    Am   G7
I need somebody with a human touch.
    C   Bb
    Hey you, al - ways on the run,
        Am   G7   C
Gotta slow it down baby, gotta have some fun. ___